Introduction to Programr

Other titles in this series

Applications in Business Data Processing
Carol Beech and Janice Burn

Business Information Systems
Chris Clare and Peri Loucopoulos

Computer Architecture and Communications
Neil Willis

Information Analysis
Janice Burn and Mike O'Neil

Software: Its Design, Implementation and Support
David Hatter, David Leigh and Roy Newton

THE COMPUTER STUDIES SERIES

Introduction to Programming

Jeff Naylor

Series Editor: David Hatter

Paradigm

Paradigm Publishing Ltd.
Avenue House
131-133 Holland Park Avenue
London W11 4UT

© Jeff Naylor 1987

First published in Great Britain 1987

British Library Cataloguing in Publication Data
Naylor, Jeff
  Introduction to programming. —— (The
  Computer studies series)
  1. Electronic digital computers —— Programming
  I. Title   II. Series
  005 . 1   QA76 . 6

  ISBN 0–948825 45 6

Typeset in 10/12pt Linotron Times by MCL Computerset Limited and printed and bound
in Great Britain by Hollen Street Press Ltd, Slough, Berks.

To Adam, Ruth and Laura

Contents

1 The programming environment   1

1.1   Introduction   1
1.2   The computer in society   1
1.3   What is programming?   3
1.4   Computer hardware   4
1.5   Programming languages and language translators   11
1.6   Software and operating systems   14
1.7   Summary   21

2 Methodical programming   23

2.1   Introduction   23
2.2   Programming skills   24
2.3   Program development cycle   25
2.4   Programs and algorithms   28
2.5   Algorithm description   30
2.6   Structured design   32
2.7   Diagrammatic notation for structured design   35
2.8   An example of structured design   37
2.9   Summary   41
2.10   Exercises   41

3 Control structures   42

3.1   Introduction   42
3.2   Leading decision loops   42
3.3   Trailing decision loops   51
3.4   Nested loops   53
3.5   Nested selection   59
3.6   Summary   65
3.7   Exercise   65

4 Simple data structures 66

4.1 Introduction 66
4.2 Fundamental classification of data 66
4.3 Numeric data types 67
4.4 Non-numeric data types 75
4.5 Structured data 79
4.6 Summary 93
4.7 Exercises 93

5 Debugging and testing 95

5.1 Introduction 95
5.2 Testing the program design 95
5.3 Syntax and syntax errors 98
5.4 Debugging 102
5.5 Testing 108
5.6 Hints on debugging and testing 110
5.7 Summary 111
5.8 Exercises 112

6 A method of structured design 113

6.1 Introduction 113
6.2 What is a structured program? 114
6.3 Data structures 115
6.4 From data structures to program structures 120
6.5 Schematic logic 132
6.6 Summary 134

7 Advanced data structures 136

7.1 Introduction 136
7.2 Physical and logical data structures 136
7.3 Linear lists 137
7.4 Trees 155
7.5 Records 162
7.6 Files 163
7.7 Summary 164
7.8 Exercises 165

8 Program implementation problems and solutions 166

8.1 Introduction 166

8.2   Structure clashes   166
8.3   Program inversion   171
8.4   Recognition problems   179
8.5   Summary   184
8.6   Exercise   185

9   Program documentation   186

9.1   Introduction   186
9.2   The purpose of documentation   186
9.3   The components of documentation   191
9.4   Documentation within the program listing   198
9.5   The provision of documentation   200
9.6   Summary   201

10   The future of programming   202

10.1   Introduction   202
10.2   Classification of languages   202
10.3   Program design versus coding   205
10.4   Fourth generation languages   209
10.5   Summary   212

Index   213

About the book

The main aim of this book is to develop a thorough understanding of the principles and practices of programming. It is particularly suitable for students taking BTEC Higher National Certificate and Diploma courses in computer studies, or degree courses in computer studies and computing science. The intention is to lay the foundation of program design and implementation so that students may subsequently develop their skills to an acceptable professional standard. No previous knowledge of programming or computers is assumed.

The book is not intended to provide a complete mastery of any one particular programming language. However, in order to emphasise the fact that programming is essentially a practical discipline, two commonly used and widely available languages (Pascal and COBOL) are used to illustrate the methods and techniques introduced. For a complete and detailed description of these two languages, the reader is referred to the appropriate language texts.

Chapter 1 introduces the reader to the program development environoment. The function of programming and the facilities that can be provided by operating systems, language translators and text editors are considered, though the treatment is at a fairly superficial level.

The design of algorithms is presented in Chapters 2 and 3, making use of a design aid which is a simplification of standard structured programming techniques.

Chapter 4 covers the use and implementation of simple data structures as gradually more complex algorithms are introduced. Throughout this part of the book, standard Pascal is used to facilitate appropriate practical examples.

Chapter 5 deals with the time-consuming activities of debugging and testing, and contains a set of hints for the novice programmer.

Emphasis is thus placed on the design and implementation of programs associated with problems commonly encountered by professional programmers. Extended examples are used in Chapters 6 and 8 to introduce a widely used professional method of program design: Jackson Structured

Programming (JSP). Chapter 7 covers advanced data structures. In this latter part of the book, the language COBOL is used to provide suitable examples of the methods being applied.

Chapter 9 deals with the often neglected topic of program documentation by means of an extended example.

The book concludes with some deliberations on the future of programming and the implications for programmers.

Throughout the book, emphasis is placed on the development of practical skills. Most chapters contain appropriate exercises by which progress may be assessed.

About the series

This series of books is the first which presents an integrated approach to the complete range of topics needed by students of Computer Studies who are currently on the Higher National Certificate and Diploma courses or the first two years of a degree course.

Each volume has been so designed through its approach and treatment of a particular subject area to stand alone: at the same time the books in the series together give a comprehensive and integrated view of computing with special attention devoted to applications in business and industry.

The authors are experienced teachers and practitioners of computing and are responsible for the design of computing syllabuses and courses for the Business and Technician Education Council, the British Computer Society and the Council for National Academic Awards. In addition many of them are members of the appropriate boards of studies for the three organisations. Their combined experience in computing practice covers all aspects of the subject.

The series presents a uniform and clear treatment of the subject and will fit well into the syllabuses of the great majority of undergraduate courses.

Acknowledgements

The contents of this book are largely derived from lecture courses I have given at North Staffordshire Polytechnic and Thames Polytechnic. I am grateful to my colleagues at both these institutions, and also to the many students who unknowingly acted as guinea pigs for the material.

A special acknowledgement must go to Philip Bradley at North Staffordshire Polytechnic, who developed the diagrammatic notation on which are based the structure diagrams introduced in Chapter 2.

I am also grateful to the Series Editor, Dave Hatter, for his constant advice and encouragement throughout the preparation of the text.

Finally, I would like to acknowledge the debt I owe to Alison Burrows, without whose patience and support this book could never have been completed.

CHAPTER 1

The programming environment

1.1 Introduction □ 1.2 The computer in society □ 1.3 What is programming? □ 1.4 Computer hardware □ 1.5 Programming languages and language translators □ 1.6 Software and operating systems □ 1.7 Summary

1.1 Introduction

This chapter attempts to set the scene for the rest of the book by describing the environment in which the programmer works. Programming is not a craft which can be practiced in isolation, it involves organising the resources of a computer to solve a particular problem. This chapter describes the characteristics of some of the most common computer resources, both hardware and software, and explains their advantages and drawbacks for various applications. Without a sound understanding of the capabilities of the computer on which he is working, a programmer cannot hope to write effective programs.

1.2 The computer in society

Computers have intruded into the life of every one of us in the 'developed' part of the world. When purchasing a can of beans at a supermarket the bar-code may be read by light pen at the checkout and the purchase recorded so that stock levels can be updated. On a train journey, the progress of the train along its route will be recorded so that signals and points can be set correctly and the train's schedule maintained. Cash dispensers set in bank walls can check the state of our accounts before handing over the money. The thickness of sheet steel passing through a rolling mill is continuously monitored so that the pressure between the

rollers can be varied to produce steel of the required thickness. These are all activities from our everyday lives and in each one of them a computer is likely to play a vital role.

Whether or not an individual will welcome the intrusion of the computer will depend very much on the individual's viewpoint. Nowadays, computers will perform the routine tasks which were boring and prone to error when done by hand, e.g. calculation of bank statements, payslips and telephone bills. Few people would object to these mundane tasks being passed to the computer. Most of us appreciate the cheap but extremely accurate watches we now carry around, based not on balance wheels and high precision engineering but on silicon chip technology and software engineering. Medical science owes a debt to the computer for making possible such significant achievements as body scanners. This author will be eternally grateful to a word processing package in a popular personal computer which aided in the development of this book. The use of computers is becoming ever more widespread, and in general terms can be seen to be improving the standard of life for the vast majority of people. It is also true, however, that the use of computers has introduced new constraints of conformity and uniformity which, for a particular individual, may be hard to accept. The assertion that the use of the computer will reduce the size of the required workforce has been shown to be largely a myth, but it has to some extent changed the nature of the required workforce. A person whose skills were previously highly valued, may now find himself in possession of the wrong skills for today's needs.

All the evidence suggests that the use of computers will continue to grow at ever increasing speed. Computers are not being used merely to replace existing manual systems with computerised systems exhibiting better efficiency and responsiveness. Brand new applications are being developed whose very existence would not be possible without the computer. Life-like simulations of activities such as driving a motor car or piloting a space craft have on the one hand allowed drivers and pilots to acquire the skills in safety, and on the other hand provided untold enjoyment for the aficionados of electronic games. The school leavers of the early 1980s were the first generation whose formal education had a significant amount of computing; to them there is nothing mysterious about a computer. Most older people, however, understand little about computers and find the computerised society a frightening prospect. The exact nature of future society is not predictable but what is certain is that we must all, irrespective of age, come to terms with the role of the computer in our society. The only way to achieve this is to understand what a computer is, and what it can do for us.

1.3 What is programming?

In very simple terms, a computer accepts data, processes that data in some prescribed way, and produces information.

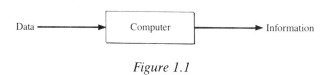

Figure 1.1

Data is the term given to all the facts, figures and events of our everyday lives. A piece of data might be a person's name, an article code number, the measured thickness of a piece of steel, the temperature of the water in a washing machine, or the event of a train passing a particular point on its route. Pieces of data related to each other are often collected into *files*. For instance, an organisation would keep an employee file of data related to its employees.

Information, on the other hand, is the result of processing or selecting from one or more files of data. Information might be a list of the names of people of a certain age, the number of articles left in stock at the end of a day's trading, the pressure required between two rollers in a steel rolling mill, the decision to switch off the heater in a washing machine, or the decision to change the setting of a signal on a railway line. If the information is destined for people, then it should be presented in an easy-to-read, well designed layout. Sometimes, the information produced by processing one set of data becomes itself the data for another process, in which case it may be presented in a more concise, perhaps encripted, format.

The computer is merely a machine capable of storing, retrieving, selecting and processing data in some prescribed manner to produce information. The manner of this processing is determined by a computer program. Without a program to instruct it, a computer is useless. The correct approach to the design and construction of good programs is the subject of the rest of this book.

Before tackling the problems of program design, it is useful to consider the nature of programming as an occupation. The first thing to note is that programming is enjoyable, even entertaining. Part of its attraction is based on the sheer pleasure experienced by most people of being able to build something, particularly something which is recognised as being useful to other people. For many people, programming also holds a certain intellectual attraction because the building material used by programmers is essentially abstract; a program can be created out of nothing, held precariously as a set of electrical signals, and equally effortlessly be destroyed. Such is the attraction of programming for some people that they become addicted to it, sitting for hours at a keyboard waiting for inspiration. The term 'hacker' is often used to describe programmers afflicted in this way. Such people usually make inefficient use of their own time and of their computer's time. A more organised, methodical approach to program design and development is just as rewarding, probably more so. One of the intentions of this book is to induce programmers to adopt such an organised approach.

1.4 Computer hardware

A program embodies the programmer's solution to a particular data processing problem. Before a programmer can begin to design the solution to a problem, he must understand the capabilities and limitations of the tools he has available for carrying out the processes involved in data processing. One major grouping of such tools is the computer hardware. Although it is not the intention of this book to examine in detail the individual hardware components and explain how they operate at the engineering or electronic level, it is necessary to look at them at the functional level. The functional characteristics of hardware components provide the constraints within which the solution to a problem must be designed.

Since a computer is used to accept raw data, store and process data in some prescribed way, and output information, it follows that the hardware

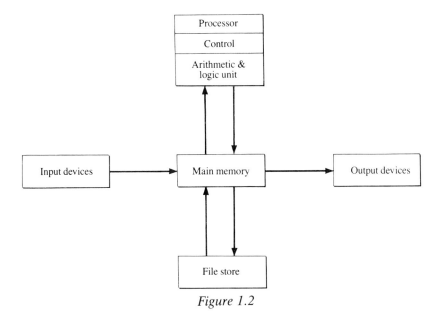

Figure 1.2

must include components capable of carrying out these functions. The hardware of every digital computer consists of

● A processor, for calculation, comparison and control
● A file store, for the temporary or permanent storage of data
● A variety of peripheral devices, for accepting raw data and presenting information

Figure 1.2 shows the components of a typical digital computer system.

The principles of operation of digital computers have changed little since electronic computers were first invented. The first computer worked on by this author was an English Electric DEUCE (Digital Electronic Universal Computing Engine). The antiquity of this name should not be taken to imply great age, merely that our perception of computers has changed considerably in a relatively short time! The DEUCE computer was physically large: rows of metal racks holding many thousands of valves (vacuum tubes) for the processor, mercury-filled delay lines for storage, and an operator's control panel containing oscilloscopes and hundreds of switches and flashing lights. The engineer actually walked inside the processor to repair it. Input/output was via paper tape. While DEUCE was physically large, the speed at which it could obey (or execute) a program, that is, its computing power, was low by modern standards. An informal unit of measurement of computers might be the power-per-cubic-foot (pcf). While the principles of operation of computer hardware have remained largely unchanged, technological advances have dramatically increased the pcf.

1.4.1 The processor

The processor, sometimes called the central processing unit (CPU) or order code processor (OCP), is the unit that actually performs the calculations and comparisons. Conventionally, it consists of three parts:

(1) *Immediate access storage.* So that the computer can gain rapid access to the program it is executing, the program itself is located in the immediate access storage. The data on which the program is currently working is also held here. Physically, the immediate access storage consists of a large number of binary digits or bits. Normally, bits are collected into groups of 8 called bytes, each capable of holding a character or (part of) a number. The size of an immediate access store varies considerably from one computer to another, but is normally in the range of 16K to 16M characters, where K = 1024 and M =1,048,576. Most immediate access stores nowadays are made from semiconductor technology, though a few are still based on ferrite cores.

(2)   *Arithmetic unit.* The arithmetic unit is that part of the processor that carries out the operations of addition, multiplication, comparison, etc. In simple terms, it is like an electronic calculator but capable of operating at much higher speeds, over one million operations per second.

(3)   *Control unit.* The control unit maintains overall control of the machine and selects, interprets and causes to be executed the instructions contained in a program. The control unit causes the computer to work slavishly in a cycle, as follows:

● The control unit fetches the next instruction from the immediate access store
● The instruction is decoded in the control unit and a pattern of electronic signals is generated
● These electronic signals trigger the immediate access storage, the arithmetic unit or one of the peripheral devices to carry out the instruction
● The whole cycle repeats from the first step.

In this way, very fast computers are capable of executing in the order of one million instructions per second. Obviously. the instructions of a program must be laid down by the programmer. The order in which the control unit selects and analyses instructions is controlled by a sequence register (or program counter), which is part of the control unit. Unless specifically told to do otherwise, by a special instruction, the sequence register selects instructions in the order in which they appear in the program.

1.4.2 The file store

Immediate access store is very fast and very compact, but it is also very expensive and limited in capacity. In many industrial data processing applications, particularly those involving process control, there is an absolute requirement for high-speed storage. Provided that the capacity requirements are not too great, immediate access storage is the obvious answer. In commercial data processing, however, large volumes of data are commonly involved and there is not normally a requirement for very high-speed access to data. Computers designed for commercial data processing are normally provided with backing (or external) storage to supplement and complement their internal immediate access storage.

Various types of backing store exist, but practically all of them use the same method for recording the data – the same method as used in the domestic cassette recorder – a moving magnetic surface on which binary data can be stored by means of magnetic polarity. Data is stored and retrieved by the use of read/write heads, positioned very close to the magnetic surface, which can convert electrical pulses into a magnetic field and vice versa. To a large extent, the rates of transfer on such devices are governed by the mechanical problems of keeping the recording surface correctly in motion. While still extremely fast by human standards, these rates of transfer are considerably slower than those that can be achieved by internal immediate access storage.

The two forms of backing store that a programmer is most likely to use are magnetic tape and magnetic disk. In a given program, the instructions which access a tape or a disk may differ only slightly from each other; indeed, they might not differ at all. However, the differences in functional characteristics of tapes and disks may have a fundamental effect on the feasibility of a proposed solution to a problem and may govern the overall design of a program.

Magnetic tape

Data is recorded on reels of magnetic tape by means of a tape deck. The domestic cassette recorder, as used with most home computers, operates in much the same way but has a less sophisticated mechanism. Tape decks on professional computers operate at higher speeds and use larger tapes (typically 2400 feet long and ½ inch wide). The total capacity of a typical reel of tape might be 20 million characters and its transfer rate might be 100,000 characters per second.

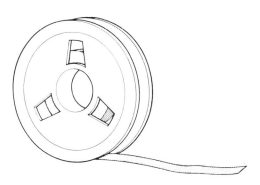

Figure 1.3

Because of the physical nature of the tape, data is recorded serially along it and must be retrieved serially. This does not present a problem when the data is naturally processed in a serial fashion, as in a large number of commercial data processing applications, but serves to exclude tapes from consideration where programs need to access data in a random order.

Magnetic disk

There is now a wide variety of magnetic disk devices which can be connected to a computer, the two most common are shown in Figure 1.4.

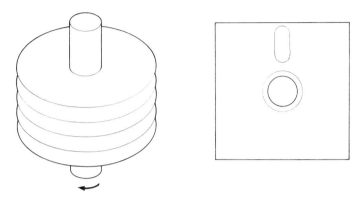

Figure 1.4

In a disk pack, disks are mounted on a central spindle in a disk drive and rotated like a gramophone record, but much faster. There may be any number between one and twenty disks mounted on a single spindle and disks may be either fixed in the drive or removable as a pack. A large replaceable disk pack might be capable of storing up to 1000M characters.

A floppy disk, as used on most personal computers, is a single disk of recording material rotated inside a protective sleeve, the recording surface being accessible through a window. A floppy disk might hold between 200K and 1M characters.

Data is recorded in concentric circles called tracks. Only the fastest disk drives have one read/write head per track; most disk drives have a small number of read/write heads, mounted on radial arms, which have to be moved to the required position. When accessing a disk, it is possible to move from one surface to another and from one track to another in any sequence. It is therefore possible to process data in any order, as appropriate to the particular application.

Each magnetic tape or disk pack is likely to contain more than one file of data, and each file may be larger than the immediate access storage available to the programmer. Programs can only make use of data when it is in immediate access storage and consequently programs have to be organised to process a file one *record* at a time. A record is a convenient grouping of individual items of data which are related to each other in some way. For instance, each record on an employee file would contain the data relating to an individual employee.

- Employee number
- Employee name
- Pay rate
- Tax code
- Etc.

Each individual item of data, for example, tax code, is known as a *field* within the record. Typically, records range in size from a few tens of characters to a few thousands of characters.

Data is transferred between immediate access store and backing store in units called *blocks* and, in terms of hardware efficiency, the larger the block the better. The convenient size for a record, in terms of the program, may be much smaller than the convenient size for a block, in terms of the hardware. In such cases, the programmer may decide to group several records together into each block. This implies the existence in immediate access store of a *buffer* for each file, where records are stored as they are processed one at a time.

The format of a block on magnetic tape is shown in Figure 1.5.

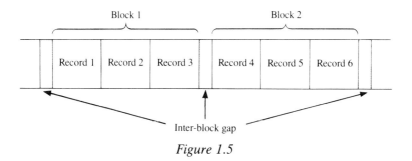

Figure 1.5

Data can only be accessed when the tape is moving at the correct speed, and the tape must be brought to a stop after each block is read or written. The interblock gap, in practice about ½ inch long, is to allow for this deceleration and acceleration. Therefore, the longer the block the more efficient is the use of the tape. A magnetic disk does not need the interblock gaps since it rotates at a constant speed, typically 2400 rpm. However, each block transfer has associated overheads: latency time (that is, waiting for the required block to appear beneath the read/write heads), and perhaps positioning time (that is, moving the read/write heads to above the required track). So again, the larger the block the more efficient is the use of the disk. The reader should be aware that other factors influence the choice of block size; for example, the maximum capacity of a track on a disk. Moreover, the larger the block, then the larger the buffer needed in immediate access store.

1.4.3 Peripheral devices

Data is record on magnetic tapes and disks in machine-readable format: a pattern of magnetic flux. The input of raw data and the output of results of a program are normally performed by devices which handle data in human-readable form. The two most common peripheral devices used by a programmer are the visual display unit and the line printer.

The visual display unit (VDU)

A VDU consists of a keyboard and a display screen, as shown in Figure 1.6

Figure 1.6

The keyboard is normally a standard QWERTY keyboard plus a few extra keys used to select the special facilities of the particular VDU. The screen, which may be monochrome or colour, of a typical VDU will be able to display about 20 lines of text, with 80 characters in each line. Each line of text represents a VDU record. As each character is keyed on the keyboard it is displayed on the screen. Successive characters keyed are either sent to the processor one at a time, or are collected in a buffer internal to the VDU and sent when the whole record has been assembled. In either case, the input of a data record is not considered complete until the RETURN key is depressed. The program waiting for the input data will not act on it until RETURN is keyed. A VDU will continue to display the last 20 lines entered. The speed of input is determined by the speed of typing. The speed of output can vary from 10 characters per second (which looks painfully slow) to over 400 characters per second (which is too fast if more than a screen-full is being output), depending on the nature of the connection to the processor. For program development, a VDU is inadequate on its own since all the screen information is lost when the VDU is switched off. A programmer will usually need to use a hard-copy device, perhaps a small printer attached to the VDU or a separate line printer.

The line printer

For medium and large computers, several types of line printer are commonly used: barrel printers, chain printers, ink-jet printers and laser printers. Speeds range from 300 to 2000 lines per minute, and such printers are very expensive. Dot-matrix printers and daisywheel printers, intended mainly for small computers, are much cheaper and much slower (up to 50 lines per minute). The number of characters per line varies from as few as 10 for some dot-matrix printers to 160; the most common line size for commercial computers is 132. The paper used is normally continuous fanfold stationery, each page holding about 60 lines of text. The smaller, slower printers normally offer more choice than the fast printers with regard to character spacing, line spacing, and even character font.

1.5 Programming languages and language translators

When a program is being executed, it is stored in binary form as a sequence of machine instructions. One by one these machine code instructions are selected by the control unit, analysed and executed. Individually, machine code instructions are very simple in their effect. The following are typical examples:

● Copy the contents of one location into another location
● Add together the contents of two locations and deposit the result in a third location
● Read an item of data from an input device and deposit it in a specified location
● Compare the contents of two locations against each other, and remember the result.
● If the result of a previous comparison was equality, then change the sequence register to a particular value

The number of bits used to encode a machine instruction varies from one machine code to another, and even from one instruction to another within the same machine code, but 32 bits is a common length.

Very early programs were written in this pure binary form. Figure 1.7 show what a binary machine-code program looked like.

```
0101001000000010001001010010011 0
0010010000100010001001110010010 1
1100010100000010001001110010100 0
1010110100000000110011 01
0101001000000010010100100000000 0
0010010000100001001001010010100 1
                    .
                    .
                    .
                  etc.
```

Figure 1.7

Programming directly in machine code had some obvious drawbacks.

● It was prone to error.
● It was very difficult to 'read', even for the programmer who wrote it, but especially for another programmer who had to modify it.
● It was very tedious and time-consuming, and therefore expensive in terms of programmer time.
● Programs could only be used on the machine for which they had been written, since all machine codes were different.

Various developments soon eased the problems of programming. Firstly, programmers were allowed to use a more convenient number base than binary—octal, decimal or hexadecimal were variously available. But these were quickly superseded by the use of symbols or mnemonics instead of numbers, giving rise to a type of programming language known as *assembly language*. A possible assembly language sequence for the binary machine code of Figure 1.7 is shown in Figure 1.8.

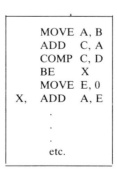

```
        MOVE A, B
        ADD   C, A
        COMP C, D
        BE    X
        MOVE E, 0
    X,  ADD   A, E
          .
          .
          .
        etc.
```

Figure 1.8

Assembly languages are described as *low-level languages* since each assembly language instruction is at the same level as the machine code instruction. Before an assembly language can be executed, however, it has to be encoded into binary. This relatively straightforward task is performed by an *assembler*. An assembler is a program written and supplied by the manufacturer of the computer; its input data is a program written in assembly language and its output is the equivalent machine code program.

Assembly language instructions are just as primitive as machine code instructions, and programs written in assembly code are still prone to error, tedious to write, difficult to read and modify, and machine dependent. *High-level languages* attempt to alleviate, if not remove, all of these problems by allowing the solution to a problem to be expressed in a language close to that used to specify the problem. Literally thousands of high-level languages have been invented over the years, but only a handful are in common use. The high-level languages Pascal and COBOL are used in illustrations throughout this book. Possible sections of Pascal and COBOL coding for the machine code of Figure 1.7 are given in Figures 1.9 and 1.10, respectively.

```
A := B;
C := C + A;
IF C < > D THEN
    E := 0;
A := A + E;

    .
    .
    .
```

Figure 1.9

```
MOVE  B TO A.
ADD  A TO C.
IF  C   NOT EQUAL D
        MOVE ZERO TO E.
ADD  E TO A.

    .
    .
    .
```

Figure 1.10

English might be considered to be the ultimate high-level language, then we could all be programmers and we would not have to read books like this! English is an extremely rich language, particularly well suited to descriptive passages and the communication of ideas and concepts. A sequence of instructions specified in English is frequently imprecise, incomplete and occasionally ambiguous. We can make sense of such sequences because of our ability to interpret, to 'read between the lines'. When we have developed the same ability inside our computers, perhaps we will then see English used as a programming language. Until then, we must use high-level languages which combine the readability of English with the formal structure and precision of assembly languages.

Each instruction in a high-level language is much more powerful than a machine code instruction. A single instruction from a high-level language may be the equivalent of a sequence of fifty or more machine code instructions. The programmer enjoys the convenience of a high-level language for the expression of his program, but it must be converted into machine code before the computer can actually execute it. This conversion is performed by a *compiler*, itself a program written and supplied by the manufacturer of the computer. The process of compilation is much more complex than the process of assembly, though the overall objective is the same: the conversion of a program into machine code. A second function of a compiler or assembler is to check that the original program conforms to the rules of the language and, if it does not, to produce suitable error messages. The general title *language translator* includes both assemblers and compilers. The process of language translation is shown diagrammatically in Figure 1.11.

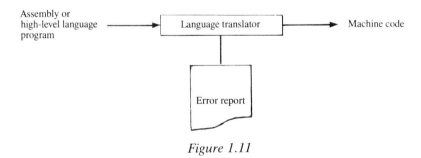

Figure 1.11

1.6 Software and operating systems

The complete collection of programs which is run on a particular computer forms its *software*. Some programs are written by the users of the computer; other programs, like language translators, are written and supplied by the manufacturer of the computer. The term *systems software* is frequently used to identify the manufacturer-written software and to distinguish it from user-written *applications software*. Sometimes, the systems software is supplied free by the manufacturer; more often nowadays the user must pay separately for each piece of systems software he wishes to use. The situation is complicated by the existence of *software houses* which offer to supply systems software in competition with computer manufacturers.

The ratio between systems software and applications software varies considerably from one computer installation to another. Some users write hardly any programs of their own, relying instead on standard applications software bought as a *software package*. Computer manufacturers and software houses again compete against each other for the provision of applications software. In some installations there are very specific require-ments and only a small amount of specialised systems software is needed. For instance, if all program development is carried out in only one high-level language, then only one language translator need be bought. However narrow the field of activities of a computer installation, there is still a need for a minimum subset of systems software in order to support the operation of the computer. This minimum subset is normally called the *operating system*.

1.6.1 Operating systems

There are different opinions of the definition of what an operating system is and what it does. In very general terms, an operating system is that part of the systems software which controls and manages the hardware, and presents to the user the facilities of the hardware in a convenient and usable form. An operating system is a necessary part of every computer, from a giant mainframe to a small personal computer.

The size of a particular operating system depends on the sophistication and the variety of services provided. A single-user system, such as a small personal computer, requires only a simple operating system. Such a user has exclusive access to all the computer's resources, and can use those resources without regard to any other users. This approach leads to an inefficient use of the computer's resources when the user's resource needs are only a small subset of the computer's resource capabilities. The cost to a user of using a computer can be reduced if he is willing to relinquish exclusive access and share the computer with other users. The sharing of resources among a number of concurrent users is the approach adopted on all but the smallest computers. The management of resources is the central function of an operating system.

Utility programs are not normally considered part of the operating system. Their main functions are to convert the medium (for example, tape to disk), sequence (for example, sorting and merging) or layout (for example, encoding and decoding) of data and programs.

Nowadays, language translators are also considered to be outside the operating system. However, there are many examples of systems where the compiler and operating system are so integrated that it is impossible to identify a clear dividing line. This applies in particular to computer systems offering only one language. In modern computer systems, it is common for all the language translators to interface to the operating system in the same way, and the functions of each are more easily distinguishable.

In slightly more specific terms, the features provided by an operating system are as follows.

(1)   *Sharing hardware among users.* Certain hardware components, such as a magnetic tape drive, cannot be switched rapidly from one user to another. Other components, such as a magnetic disk drive, can normally be switched in a matter of milliseconds. The operating system must have policies, appropriate to each component type, for allocating and deallocating the hardware among the various users.

(2)   *Scheduling resources among users.* Where a resource can be switched quickly between users, the operating system must decide the order in which users are allocated the resource. This applies to certain hardware components like the central processing unit, and also to software resources like language translators.

(3)   *Controlling the sharing of data between users.* In certain circumstances, it is feasible, even desirable, for two or more users to share access to the same data, held either in immediate access storage or backing storage. The operating system must provide mechanisms for allowing this sharing while at the same time ensuring the privacy of non-shared data.

(4)   *Defining user interface.* In order for the facilities of a system to be provided to a user, the user must communicate his resource needs to the operating system. This is done via a *command language* or a *job control language*, more about which will be said later in this section.

(5)   *Facilitating input/output.* With several users using a system simultaneously, it is necessary that the use of the input/output facilities be centrally coordinated and controlled. Moreover, the operating system provides the low-level control of input/output devices and thus allows user programs to specify an input/output operation in a symbolic, high-level way.

(6)   *Detecting and recovering from errors.* Throughout the operation of a computer system, the operating system is monitoring activity to detect errors in hardware or software. When such an error is detected, the operating system will try to correct the problem or at least minimise the damage to the users of the system.

Different operating systems have different design philosophies. The importance placed on each individual feature, and the way in which each individual feature is presented to the user, will differ from one operating system to another. An operating system will attempt to create a particular

possible, or even intended, to maximise the utilisation of the computer's resources. However, an interactive environment is accepted as being the most effective for the programmer, in terms of minimising the total program development time. Nearly all programmers now work in interactive environments.

The distinction between batch processing and interactive systems is sometimes difficult to draw. Some systems offer the programmer an interactive environment throughout the editing phase but then deal with requests for compilation and execution by batch processing. Other systems extend the interactive environment to include the compilation but revert to batch processing for the execution. Whenever the switchover occurs, the programmer can then turn his attention to another program or simply leave the terminal and await the results. Where the turnaround time is predictably fast, some systems allow the programmer to wait at the terminal for his program to finish execution and then display the results on the screen.

It is possible to connect a terminal to an interactive system over a considerable distance. Indeed, many such connections are made over ordinary telephone lines. This widens the access to the computer but presents problems of security. To ensure that only authorised users can gain access to a computer's facilities, it is necessary for a user to identify himself by *logging in* or *logging on*. This consists of a short dialogue where the user answers questions posed by the computer. The answer to each question is checked against a list of acceptable answers. Only if the user negotiates the sequence correctly does he gain access to the system. A typical dialogue is shown in Figure 1.13, the computer in italics.

```
Login      Jeff
Account    Pitman
Password   Mysecret
Welcome to the XYZ computer service
        Logging in at 11.18 on Friday 5th March 1985
        Have a nice day
```

Figure 1.13

In response to *Login* the user types a name or identifier which is unique to him. *Account* identifies who pays for the facilities about to be used. The response to *Password* is a secret word associated with the user's identifier but known only to the user and the computer. As the user types his password, the computer suppresses its printing on the VDU screen to help maintain the secrecy. If you know a person well it is surprisingly easy to guess what he would choose as a password. Users are advised to change their passwords fairly frequently. At the end of a successful logging in dialogue, it is normal for the computer to display a welcoming message plus any other useful information. For instance, the user could be warned if the interactive service was about to be withdrawn to allow for machine maintenance.

At the end of the interactive session, the user must inform the computer that he has finished by *logging out* or *logging off*. A typical sequence is shown in Figure 1.14.

Logout
User Jeff logged out at 11.45 on Friday 5th March 1985
Connect time 27 minutes
Debited to account Pitman

Figure 1.14

The computer acknowledges the logging out request, and displays a summary of accounting information.

1.6.4 Text editors and formatters

An important and time-consuming phase within the program development cycle is the amending of an incorrect source program to produce a correct version. Programs, like data, are permanently stored in files in some type of backing storage on a medium which is not human-readable. A text editor is a program which offers the user easy manipulation and amendment of the contents of a file; whether the file contains a program or raw data is largely irrelevant. Text editors are part of the systems software supplied by the computer manufacturer, but normally not considered part of the operating system. Some text editors are designed for use with only a single programming language, typically BASIC, and are highly integrated with the language translator. More common nowadays, and much more useful to the professional programmer, are general purpose editors which can be applied to any text file, whether it contains a Pascal program, a COBOL program, or raw data.

The operation of a text editor is shown in Figure 1.15.

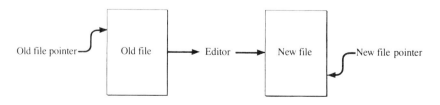

Figure 1.15

The contents of the old file are transcribed to the new file, with any necessary insertions, deletions or amendments being performed by the editor. The editor maintains a pointer to each file, identifying the position that editing has reached. Normally, the two pointers start at the first record, or line, of their respective file and proceed sequentially through the file. Some advanced editors, however, allow the user to move the old file pointer backwards and forwards though the file in order to access the lines in any sequence and achieve special editing effects.

Early *line editors* functioned at the record level; it was only possible to insert, delete or replace a complete line at a time. More modern *context editors*, however, allow the user to identify and process individual characters or strings of characters within a file. For instance, it is possible to ask the editor to find and display the next occurrence in the file of a particular string of characters. Most editors allow the user the choice of line numbers or character strings as the means of positioning the old file pointer. *Screen editors* display a screen-full, or page, of the file at a time and alterations are made by positioning the VDU's cursor and overtyping with the required characters. The programmer moves through the file a page at a time. Screen editors offer many of the facilities of word-processing systems, and they are very popular with programmers.

COBOL is an example of a language with a prescribed layout for various parts of a program; the layout of other parts of the program is left to the programmer. Pascal is an example of a free format language where the programmer has total control over the layout of his program. Even where programmers have control over format, it is normal for them to adhere to a convention to improve the readability of their program. Attempting to type in a program in a standard format is time-consuming and prone to error. A *formatter* takes a free format program and rearranges it to conform to the conventional layout. Obviously, a different formatter is normally needed for each different language, since they need to be able to recognise certain features of a language. Formatters save the programmer much time, and they can actually help him to find errors in his program by making structural problems more obvious.

1.7 Summary

In this chapter, we have considered the nature of the job of programming. We have identified and described some of the more common components of a computer system which a programmer has to understand and use in his everyday job. The capabilities of the available hardware and software have a fundamental influence on the way in which a computer can be applied to the solution of a problem. Before studying the techniques of programming, described in the following chapters, you should find out as much as you can about the computer on which you will be working. Find out how to log in, how to create files, how to invoke the compilers. Become acquainted with the keyboard you will be using, and find out where the documentation manuals are kept. You will need all this information, and more, before venturing further into this book.

CHAPTER 2

Methodical programming

2.1 Introduction □ 2.2 Programming skills □ 2.3 Program development cycle □ 2.4 Programs and algorithms □ 2.5 Algorithm description □ 2.6 Structured design □ 2.7 Diagrammatic notations for structured design □ 2.8 An example of structured design □ 2.9 Summary □ 2.10 Exercises

2.1 Introduction

As with all occupations, programming has an associated set of methods and techniques by which it is performed. When programming was in its infancy, these methods and techniques were not known, simply because no one had programmed before. As experience was gained in programming, the objectives of a good program were identified and various methods were used to achieve these objectives. Some of these methods proved successful and have survived to the present day; others proved unsuccessful and were replaced by more effective methods. Even the successful methods have been refined and improved over the years. This chapter describes the fundamental methods and techniques used by today's programmer to produce his programs.

The early part of the chapter concentrates on how the programmer divides his time between the various stages in the program development cycle: specification, design, coding, testing and maintenance. The latter part of the chapter introduces the techniques of structured program design, emphasising that errors are reduced if programming is kept simple. Various ways of describing programs are examined, and this chapter introduces a diagrammatic notation suitable for describing structured programs.

2.2 Programming skills

In Chapter 1 it was stated that a computer is merely a machine capable of storing, retrieving, selecting and processing data in order to produce information, and that the manner of this processing is determined by a computer program. Nowadays, almost all programs are written in a high-level language, for the reasons outlined in Chapter 1, and there are literally thousands of high-level languages. There are several reasons why so many different high-level languages have been invented.

(1) The nature of data, and of the processing that needs to be performed on the data, can vary considerably from one situation to another. In most cases, a programming language is designed to express the solution of a particular type of problem. For example, FORTRAN was designed to allow the mathematical manipulation of numeric data to be performed in a convenient and fast manner; COBOL was designed to facilitate the description and processing of data commonly found in business organisations; MODULA was designed to enable computerised control of real-time activities.

(2) Language designers have tended to disagree about the features of the 'best' language for a particular class of applications. Consequently, there has been a proliferation of languages which are similar to each other in broad concepts but differ from each other at the detailed level.

(3) The universal language, containing the features of all types of programming language and capable of expressing the solution of all types of problems, is still pursued by some language designers and manufacturers. PL/I is an example of such a language.

To express the solution to a particular problem in a language designed for a different class of problem is often inconvenient and sometimes impossible. However, with such a wealth of languages available it is almost inevitable that a particular program can be written in several different languages. A given computer installation may have the resources to support half a dozen different languages; a given professional programmer may have expertise in one or two languages and a working knowledge of two or three more. The skills of a professional programmer fall into two categories:

● Skills, knowledge and abilities which are specific to a given language
● Generic skills, knowledge and abilities which can be applied to a wide variety of different programming languages

These generic skills are the more important in the long term. They enable the programmer to be more adaptable to change, and make it easy for him to learn new languages. Generic programming skills also offer advantages to the employers of programmers, allowing the programmer to be treated as a flexible resource at the various stages of the program development cycle.

2.3 Program development cycle

In a typical data processing department, many programmers will be employed. On anything other than trivial programs, it is common for programmers to work in teams. A programming team allocated to a large software project may find itself developing several different programs in parallel. The progress in the development of each program and the workload placed on each individual programmer must be carefully monitored. To facilitate control of this management problem, it is normal to consider program development as separated into distinct stages.

Specification

After detailed analysis of the problem to be solved, it is necessary to draw up a detailed specification of the program, or set of programs, needed to carry out the solution. The level of detail in a program specification will vary considerably. As a minimum, it would contain details of the input and output of the program, and an outline of how the output is to be produced from the input. A detailed specification would include a step-by-step description of the action of the program. The specification itself is a written document, and frequently makes use of diagrams to elucidate the text. It is normally produced by a systems analyst, not the programmer.

Design

A detailed program design must be derived from the program specification. At this stage, the internal organisation of the program will probably be defined in some standard diagrammatic notation and will, to a large extent, remain independent of the language to be used. However, the level of detail needed in the finished program design will reflect the level of the language in which the program will be written. There is obviously a trade-off between specification and design; the more detailed the specification the less onerous the construction of the detailed design (assuming that the specification is correct).

Coding and implementation

The detailed design is converted into a program in the chosen language. If the detailed design is at the correct level, then this conversion into code is fairly painless, even mechanical. The same programmer might produce both the detailed design and the coded program. Alternatively, a less experienced programmer may be used at the coding stage. Once coded, the program must be made ready for execution on the computer. This might involve combining the program with other programs or manufacturer-written utilities which form part of the overall computerised solution.

Testing

The program is tested to determine if it conforms to the original specification. The programmer invents appropriate test data and compares the output produced by the program against the expected results. Test data should be chosen so as to test all aspects of the program specification. Each successful test of the program increases the programmer's confidence in the correctness of the program. The early stages of testing are likely to be performed by the programmer who produced the coding. Other programmers are likely to contribute to the later stages of testing so as to provide some independent assessment.

Normal operation and maintenance

The program goes into normal operation, routinely solving the problem for which it was designed. It is not uncommon for residual errors to be found at this stage, the number of errors depending on the skill of the program designer/coder and the thoroughness of program testing. The correction of these errors might involve changes to the program code, design, or original specification. The normal lifetime of a program is several years, and over this time-scale the user's requirements might easily change, necessitating changes to the specification and hence to the program. Commonly, the maintenance of an operational program is not performed by the original programmer. There is, therefore, a need to provide documentation so that programs are easily understandable. Equally important is the need for programs to be designed in such a way that they are easily adaptable.

From the above description, it should be clear that the stages in the program development cycle are not independent and easily defined. It should be equally clear that during the development of practically any program it will be necessary to repeat various parts of the development cycle. Some of the possible loops within the development cycle are shown in Figure 2.1. Program development is an iterative process of continual refinement and improvement.

The number of problems occurring during the operation and maintenance stage depends largely on the skill with which the earlier stages were performed. Indeed, the number of programmer hours, and therefore the cost, of the later stages in the cycle depend on the success of the earlier stages. The amount of programmer time spent on the operation and maintenance stage varies considerably, and depends partly on factors not controlled by the programmer: for instance, the number of changes to the user's requirements. Also, the longer a program survives before replace-

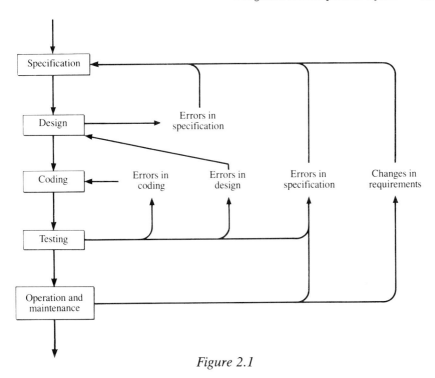

Figure 2.1

ment, the more errors will be found. The total maintenance bill can never decrease.

It is easier to analyse the first four stages of program development. Programmers are remarkably optimistic, and they write their programs as if they were going to work correctly first time. In practice, it is very rare for a non-trivial program to be written correctly at the first attempt. Even experienced programmers seem surprised at the amount of time it takes them to eliminate errors from their program. Spending more time on the planning stages (that is, specification and design) normally leads to considerably fewer problems at the testing stage and an overall reduction in time. The coding stage is certainly the easiest to predict, largely because of its mechanical nature, as mentioned earlier. In the planning of a programming project, the time for the testing stage is most frequently underestimated, particularly where large complex programs are involved. Figure 2.2 shows the allocation of programmer time between the stages of program development, as found in a typical data processing department. Many programmers are surprised that as much as half of their time is spent on the testing stage. The adoption of sensible and correct techniques during the stages of specification and design is the best way to reduce the overall time.

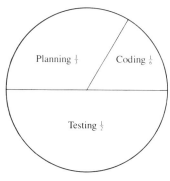

Figure 2.2

2.4 Programs and algorithms

The fact that a particular program design can be coded in a number of languages indicates that the solution of the associated problem is essentially language independent. Throughout most of the design stage of program development it is normal for the solution to be refined in language-independent terms. As the detail of the design is developed, it becomes necessary to make some consideration of the expected implementation language. This is to take advantage of special features of the chosen language and to avoid the use of techniques which are difficult to express in the chosen language. Nevertheless, it is normal for even the detailed design of a program to be specified in a way that is language-independent.

When we first start to design the solution to a problem we tend to look at the problem in a very high-level fashion: that is, we decide *what* it is we have to achieve. As we continue to consider the problem we begin to evolve a method of solution: that is, we decide *how* the objectives may be achieved. It may be that a complex problem is best solved by a collection of subprograms, all cooperating and working together to provide the overall solution. The design of each of these subprograms would start from a specification of what it has to do and finish with a description of how it is to do it. Each subprogram would handle a subproblem of the overall problem. Whether we need to resort to subprograms or not, eventually we must produce a step-by-step description of the method of solution. Such a step-by-step description is often referred to as an *algorithm*.

Although a method of solution has been found, the design stage is far from over. The method we have found may prove to be impractical, and a different method may have to be found. For instance, one way of producing perfect numbers is to take each successive positive integer, 1,2,3,... and so on, identify all its exact divisors (by checking if it is exactly divisible by any of the positive integers less than itself) and determining if the sum of these divisors is equal to the number itself. There is no doubt that this method would work, but it is a totally impractical way of finding large perfect numbers. The 23rd perfect number has 6751 digits (I think!) and using the above method even the fastest computers would not find it before the programmer had long ceased to care about perfect numbers. Even if the algorithm proves to be adequate, it may still require significant improvement.

An algorithm can be assessed for quality. The purpose of an algorithm is to describe a solution to a particular problem, and it is therefore important that an algorithm be easy to understand. Also, an algorithm which provides solutions to an entire class of problems is clearly more useful than one that is very narrow in its applicability. Similarly, it is desirable for an algorithm to be easily adapted to meet changes in the problem.

Algorithms can also be assessed for efficiency; the time taken for the execution of an algorithm, and the amount of storage space and other resources required by the algorithm being factors for consideration. In general, there is a trade-off between time and space—the faster an algorithm, the more storage space it requires.

We can now attempt a definition of an algorithm:

'An algorithm for the solution of a problem is a specification of a reasonable number of instructions such that if the instructions are obeyed then either a solution of the problem is found or it is determined that no solution exists. In either case, the algorithm terminates after a reasonable number of steps.'

Algorithms are not only used in a computing context. Knitting patterns, food recipes and model aircraft assembly instructions are just as much algorithms as are computer programs. In the above definition, the meaning of the word 'reasonable' is obviously open to interpretation. What is a reasonable number of steps to a computer may be totally unreasonable to a human being.

Within the context of this book, we are concerned with algorithms which are subsequently converted into computer programs. As might be expected, the criteria by which computer programs are assessed are strongly related to the criteria by which algorithms are assessed. The quality of a computer program is judged under the following headings.

Correctness

Does the program always function according to its specification? The correctness of a program depends on the skill with which the stages of design, coding and testing were carried out. The use of the term correctness here is intended to include reliability. The consequences of a program failing to supply reliably the correct results can vary from mild inconvenience to loss of life.

Ease of use

Is the program convenient and easy to use? When designing a program, particularly the input and output, it is vital to bear in mind the type of people who will use the program. Frequently, users have no specialist knowledge of computing. The 'friendliness' of a program is a measure of its ease of use.

Maintainability

Is the program easy to modify if any amendments become necessary? Maintenance of operational programs consumes a significant amount of programmer time. The ease with which maintenance can be carried out depends on the adaptability and generality of the program's underlying algorithms.

Portability

If the user buys new hardware, can he easily transfer his programs? Transfer of programs to a new machine can be facilitated by the use of a standard high-level language. Even then, some conversion work is normally necessary.

Efficiency

Does the program make efficient use of the computer's resources? In the extreme case, a program cannot be executed if its requirements exceed the computer's available resources. Similarly, the user may place a requirement on the speed of execution in order to maintain a given response time.

It is impossible to rank these criteria; indeed, the ranking would vary from one program to another and from one area of application to another. Without a doubt, correctness is the main requirement of a program and in some applications (for example, spacecraft control) reliable operation is as important as correct results. The importance of the efficiency criteria has gradually diminished over the years as computer processing power has increased in size and decreased in cost. Process control environments are one area where speed of response is as important as ever.

2.5 Algorithm description

There are many ways in which we could specify the solution to a problem. We could try using passages of English text, and describe the solution almost like a story. Take as an example the problem of safely crossing the road.

We all have an intuitive idea about the 'algorithm' to solve this problem. In English, we might describe it in the following simple way.

'Walk to the edge of the pavement. Look left and right. If the road is clear walk across. Otherwise do it again.'

An obvious problem is identifying what is meant by 'it' in the final sentence. An adult would probably be able to interpret the meaning from the context, a child might get confused. A better last sentence might be 'Otherwise go back to the second sentence'. Apart from being cumbersome, this approach presupposes that each separate action in the algorithm is specified in a separate sentence so that it can be referenced by other parts of the algorithm. The wide choice of words and sentence structure available in the English language makes it inherently ambiguous and unsuitable for algorithm description. The purpose of an algorithm description is to communicate the solution to a problem; the notation used for the description must not be responsible for distorted or ambiguous communication.

A notation used by many programmers is the flowchart.The flowchart notation is unambiguous and a great improvement over English text. It is also very flexible and allows algorithms to be described with a wide variety of structures and organisations. This great flexibility sometimes makes flowcharts difficult to convert into the statements available in modern programming languages. For this reason, flowcharts are no longer widely

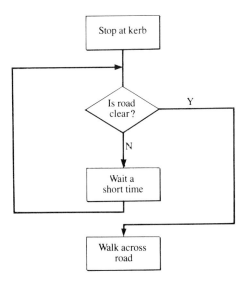

Figure 2.3

used by professional programmers and have been superseded by better methods of algorithm description.

In a flowchart, the individual steps of an algorithm are enclosed in boxes and the sequence of the steps is indicated by directed lines connecting the boxes. Differently shaped boxes are used to indicate different types of step, thus making the flowchart more readable. The two most important shapes are the rectangle, indicating an action, and the rhomboid, indicating a decision. Using a flowchart notation, the algorithm for crossing the road might appear as in Figure 2.3.

A third possible notation is pseudocode. Pseudocode allows algorithms to be described in English words but restricts the structures available to those found in modern programming languages. A pseudocode example of the algorithm to cross the road is shown in Figure 2.4.

```
Cross the road:
        stop at the curb
        while the road is not clear do
                wait a short time
        end while
        walk across the road
```

Figure 2.4

Indentation is important in pseudocode, and is used to help identify the individual structures within the pseudocode. To this extent, good pseudocode is dependent upon good formatting. Bad formatting makes pseudocode difficult to understand.

2.6 Structured design

The objective of structured design is to take the specification of a problem and from it produce an algorithm which can be easily converted into a programming language. Whatever flexibility is theoretically available during the design of an algorithm, it is obviously sensible to construct the algorithm only from structures which are themselves available explicitly in the eventual programming language. This considerably reduces the probability of errors being introduced during the coding stage by making the coding more easy to produce.

Considerations along these lines have led to the identification of three fundamental building-blocks of program construction: sequence, selection and iteration. From these three control structures alone, it is possible to construct any program. To simplify the task of programming, it is sensible to design algorithms which use only these three structures and to select programming languages which offer them.

The next three sections describe these control structures in detail. Notice that each control structure has only a single entry and a single exit, thus making it easy to link together the control structures within a program.

2.6.1 Sequence

A sequence consists of two or more components, specified in the order in which they must be obeyed. For instance, the following English sentence specifies a sequence of three components.

'First do Process A, then do Process B, and then do Process C.'

Figure 2.5 gives the flowchart and pseudocode equivalents.

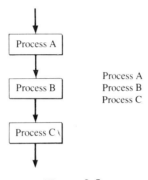

Process A
Process B
Process C

Figure 2.5

2.6.2 Selection

A selection consists of one or more components, one of which must be obeyed. The simplest form of selection is specified in the following sentence.

'If condition X is true then do Process A.'

Figure 2.6 gives the flowchart and pseudocode equivalents.

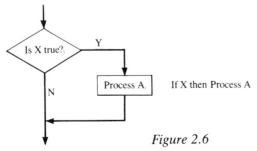

If X then Process A

Figure 2.6

Another simple form of selection is specified in the following sentence:

'If condition X is true then do Process A, otherwise do Process B.'

Figure 2.7 gives the flowchart and pseudocode equivalents.

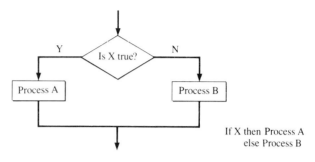

If X then Process A
else Process B

Figure 2.7

More complicated forms of selection exist, where a component of a selection may itself be a selection. They are potentially difficult to understand and have no direct equivalent in most programming languages. For the moment we will ignore them and consider them later in the book.

2.6.3 Iteration

An iteration consists of a single component which is obeyed zero or more times. A typical iteration is specified in the following sentence:

'While condition X is true, repeatedly do Process A.'

Figure 2.8 gives the flowchart and the pseudocode equivalents.

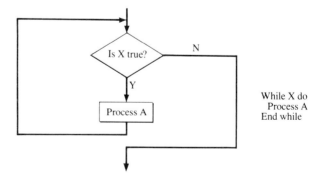

While X do
    Process A
End while

Figure 2.8

Other forms of iteration do exist, but this is arguably the best type. This form of iteration is certainly sufficient for any programming problem and we will concentrate our attention on it.

2.6.4 Stepwise refinement

For very small programs, the entire program development cycle can be completed in a matter of minutes. The method of solution may be immediately obvious. Using an appropriate notation, an algorithm could be described, desk-checked and converted into a programming language. If an interactive environment were available, the program could be keyed in and tested at a terminal. If the program failed to execute correctly, it would probably be fairly simple to spot the error, correct it and run the program again. This informal *ad hoc* approach works well with problems which can be understood and solved in a single unit. However, as the size and complexity of the problems increase, it becomes necessary to develop a methodical way of constructing programs. *Stepwise refinement* is such a methodical way, and is implicit in structured design.

The basic principle of stepwise refinement is that any non-trivial problem can be broken down (that is, refined) into a number of subproblems which can be solved separately. Each subproblem may need to be further refined, and so on. The process of refinement stops when a level of detail has been reached where each lowest level subproblem can be easily converted into the programming language. This process can also be described as top-down design, since we start with the highest level (that is, the whole problem) and work down through successive layers of increasing detail. At each layer, the program is defined as a collection of component parts related by the three fundamental control structures.

2.7 Diagrammatic notation for structured design

The three notations we have looked at for algorithm description are all inadequate in some way for structured design. English text is insufficiently concise or precise. Pseudocode is not very visual and is too reliant on good format. Flowcharts are too flexible and encourage unstructured control sequences. In this section, we introduce a structure diagram notation which has the accuracy and visual impact of flowcharts but constrains the programmer to adhere to the principles of structured design.

2.7.1 Sequence

A sequence is denoted by a vertical line to which stubs are attached, and to each stub is attached a component in the sequence. Component names are written in upper case if they are further defined elsewhere. Lower case is used for components already at the lowest level of detail. Figure 2.9 gives an example of sequence containing two lowest level components and one component, VALIDATA, for which a separate structure diagram exists elsewhere.

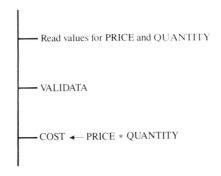

Figure 2.9

The flow of control is always from top to bottom, so no arrows are needed. Note the use of ⟵ to denote 'is assigned the value of'.

2.7.2 Selection

Figure 2.10 gives an example of the simplest form of selection and corresponds exactly to Figure 2.6.

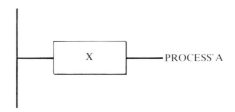

Figure 2.10

The selection element is attached via a stub to the main stem at the point at which the condition is evaluated. If the condition is true, the component attached to the stub of the selection element is executed.

The other common form of selection is shown in Figure 2.11. This corresponds exactly to Figure 2.7. Either Process A or Process B is executed, depending on the truth of condition X.

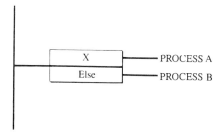

Figure 2.11

2.7.3 Iteration

Several different types of iteration are possible. An example of the type corresponding to Figure 2.8 is shown in Figure 2.12.

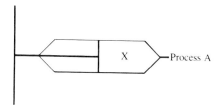

Figure 2.12

Process A is repeatedly executed while condition X remains true. If condition X is false on initial entry to the iteration element then Process A is not executed at all.

The other two parts of the iteration element are used to describe a different type of iteration, and will be introduced in the next chapter.

2.8 An example of structured design

Undoubtedly the best way to understand the process of structured design is to work through an example.

Example 2.1 Netchange program

Suppose we have a sequential input file terminated by an end-of-file record. Each data record contains two fields: an indicator field IND and an amount field NUM. We require a program which reads all the records from this input file and for each input record performs the following processing: if the IND field equals 1 the value of NUM is added to a running total

RUNTOT; if the value of IND is 2, the value of NUM is subtracted from RUNTOT. We may assume that all data records have been checked for validity. When all the data records have been processed, the value of RUNTOT (that is, the net change) is printed. Before processing any data records, the value of RUNTOT must be initialised to zero.

A possible sequence of successive refinements is given in Figures 2.13, 2.14, 2.15 and 2.16.

The first refinement broke down the problem into a sequence of three components. In the second refinement we are able to specify two of those components at the detailed level and identify that the third component, READLOOP, contains an iteration of a component PROCESSRECORD. In the third refinement we can specify the detail of PROCESSRECORD as a selection.

At each stage of refinement we only consider necessary details. Other details, which might confuse us, are ignored. Notice how the number of

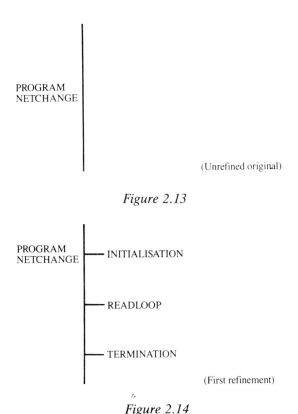

PROGRAM
NETCHANGE

(Unrefined original)

Figure 2.13

PROGRAM
NETCHANGE   ── INITIALISATION

── READLOOP

── TERMINATION

(First refinement)

Figure 2.14

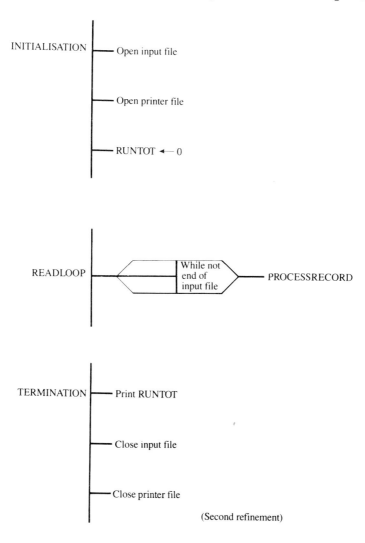

Figure 2.15

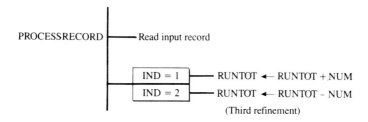

Figure 2.16

refinements required will vary from one part of the program to another. The diagrams of Figures 2.13, 2.14, 2.15 and 2.16 are sufficient to define the necessary program. Alternatively, they could be combined into a single structure diagram as in Figure 2.17.

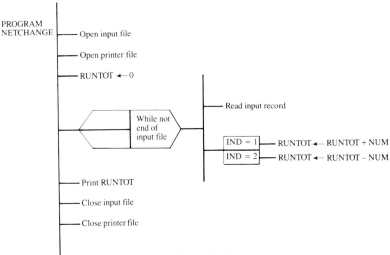

Figure 2.17

A single structure diagram for a complete program has some attractions, but as soon as we begin to consider long and complex problems a single diagram becomes impractical and even undesirable. The physical boundaries of the piece of paper on which we draw such diagrams put a convenient limit on their complexity.

To conclude this section, Figure 2.18 shows a Pascal program equivalent to the structure diagram of Figure 2.17.

```
PROGRAM NETCHANGE (INPUT, OUTPUT);
VAR RUNTOT, IND, SUM : INTEGER;
BEGIN
      RUNTOT := 0;
      WHILE NOT EOF DO
      BEGIN
            READLN (IND, NUM);
            IF IND = 1 THEN RUNTOT := RUNTOT + SUM
                       ELSE RUNTOT := RUNTOT - SUM
      END;
      WRITELN (RUNTOT)
END.
```

Figure 2.18

2.9 Summary

In this chapter, we have examined some of the methods and techniques which have become associated with the programming profession. The design and coding of programs are only part of a programmer's job, and the evidence of the last few years suggests that they are a relatively small part of the total program development cycle. This chapter has also introduced the important concepts of structured programming and stepwise refinement, the basic principles upon which almost all professional programmers base the design of their programs.

The methods and techniques described in this chapter represent what most people consider to be the 'current state of the art'. It must be remembered, however, that these methods and techniques are subject to continuous evolution, and that developments are taking place very quickly. Possible future changes in the nature of the programmer's job will be discussed in Chapter 10.

2.10 Exercises

2.10.1 Design a program to input a sequence of numbers, terminated by a zero, and print out the average, largest and smallest. Express your design in
   ● Pseudocode
   ● Flowchart
   ● Structure diagram

2.10.2 Design a program to input the coefficients of a quadratic equation and output the roots of the equation. Express your design in
   ● Pseudocode
   ● Flowchart
   ● Structure diagram

2.10.3 Design a program to calculate INCOMETAX from GROSSPAY, assuming
   ● The first £5000 is tax free
   ● The next £3000 is taxed at 35%
   ● The next £5000 is taxed at 45%
   ● The remainder is taxed at 65%
   Express your design in pseudocode, flowchart and structure diagram.

CHAPTER 3

Control structures

3.1 Introduction □ 3.2 Leading decision loops □ 3.3 Trailing decision
loops □ 3.4 Nested loops □ 3.5 Nested selections □ 3.6 Summary □
3.7 Exercise

3.1 Introduction

Sequence, selection and iteration have been introduced as the three
elements of structured design. It is possible to construct any program from
these three control structures. The first of these control structures,
sequence, is implemented very easily in both Pascal and COBOL:
statements are executed in the order in which they appear in the program
listing. The remaining two control structures, selection and iteration,
require more attention.

This chapter looks at the way selection and iteration are implemented
in Pascal and COBOL. Both languages offer various facilities for incorporating these constructs into a program and this chapter evaluates these
facilities with respect to the philosophy of structured design. The chapter
also serves to reinforce the use of stepwise refinement in the development
of a program design.

3.2 Leading decision loops

The type of iteration introduced in Section 2.6.3 of the previous chapter
is described in the flowchart and structured diagram of Figure 3.1.

This type of iteration is called a *leading decision loop*. Process A is
repeatedly executed while condition X remains true. If condition X is false
on initial entry to the iteration element then Process A is not executed at
all and no looping takes place. The leading decision loop is the most
common and, most programmers would agree, the most useful iteration

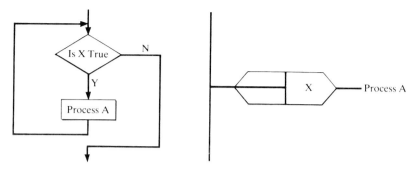

Figure 3.1

element for the construction of structured programs.

In a leading decision loop the decision leads the body of the loop and hence the body of the loop is executed zero or more times.

3.2.1 Pascal WHILE statement

The most common way of implementing a leading decision loop in Pascal is the WHILE statement. In terms of Figure 3.1, the WHILE statement has the following format.

WHILE X DO PROCESSA;

In the above example, the body of the loop is shown as a single simple statement: PROCESSA. In the general case, the body of a loop can be a sequence of simple statements, delimited by BEGIN and END, and known as a *compound statement*. For example, Figure 3.2 shows a WHILE loop where the body of the loop consists of three separate statements. PROCESSX, PROCESSY and PROCESSZ are executed sequentially but indivisibly. Before each execution of the body of the loop, the condition is re-examined to see if it is still true.

```
WHILE X DO
BEGIN
        PROCESSX;
        PROCESSY;
        PROCESSZ
END;
```

Figure 3.2

Example 3.1

Print out the cubes of all the positive integers, starting at 1, and stopping before the first cube which exceeds 100.

```
NUM   := 1;
CUBE  := 1;
WHILE CUBE <= 100 DO
BEGIN
        WRITELN (CUBE:3);
        NUM := NUM+1;
        CUBE := NUM**3
END;
```

This loop is controlled by the Boolean expression CUBE <= 100. The WHILE statement always tests the condition before executing the body of the loop. It is therefore the programmer's responsibility to ensure that the condition is correctly initialised before the WHILE statement is entered. Initialising CUBE to any integer less than or equal to 100 would have been sufficient to cause the body of the loop to be executed. It is specifically initialised to the value 1 so that it may be used to print the first number in the output. Notice that although NUM does not appear explicitly in the loop condition, its correct initialisation outside the loop and its correct incrementation inside the loop are necessary for the continuing successful operation of the loop control.

Example 3.2

Print out the cubes of the first 10 positive integers.

Here we know in advance how many times the body of the loop is to be executed, and the loop can therefore be controlled by a counter.

```
NUM := 1;
WHILE NUM <= 10 DO
BEGIN
        CUBE := NUM**3;
        WRITELN (CUBE:3);
        NUM := NUM+1
END;
```

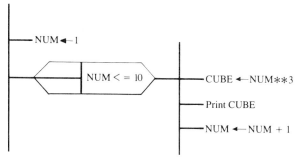

In this example, NUM is known as the *loop control variable*. It is explicitly used within the loop condition, and it must be correctly initialised before the loop and correctly modified within the loop. If the programmer forgets to modify the loop control variable within the loop, then the value of the loop condition remains unchanged and the loop body will be executed repeatedly in an *infinite loop*, assuming that the loop condition was initially true.

Example 3.3

Print out the cubes of the first N positive integers, where N is read from data.

This example is almost identical to the previous one, and uses another counter-controlled loop. The number of times the body of the loop is to be executed is not known in numeric terms, but it is known to be 'the current value of N'.

```
READ (N);
NUM := 1;
WHILE NUM <= N DO
BEGIN
        CUBE := NUM**3;
        WRITELN (CUBE:3);
        NUM := NUM+1
END;
```

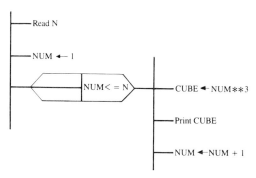

Example 3.4

Print out the cubes of the numbers read from data, the end of the data being indicated by a value of zero.

The problem here is to avoid executing the body of the loop when the special end-of-data marker, in this case zero, has been read. A straight-forward solution to this problem is to use the *read-ahead* technique. The first item of data is read outside the loop. This value is processed in the loop and the last statement in the loop reads the next item of data. Note that this approach works even if the end-of-data marker is the only item of data.

```
READ (NUM);
WHILE NUM < > 0 DO
BEGIN
        CUBE := NUM**3;
        WRITELN (CUBE:3);
        READ (NUM)
END;
```

Example 3.5

Count the number of values in the data, the end of the data being indicated by a value of zero.

When using a loop structure, it is quite common to have to count the number of times the loop is executed, perhaps in order to calculate averages.

```
COUNT := 0;
READ (NUM);
WHILE NUM < > 0 DO
BEGIN
        COUNT := COUNT+1;
        READ (NUM)
END;
```

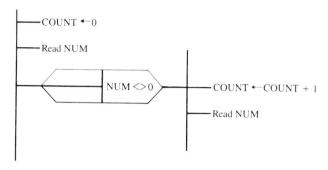

3.2.2 Pascal FOR statement

Examples 3.2 and 3.3 involve the use of counter-controlled loops. Three separate actions are performed on the loop-control variable: initialisation, testing against final value, and modification. Pascal offers a single statement which combines these three actions: the FOR statement. The FOR statement is provided merely for convenience; it can do nothing that cannot also be done by a combination of other statements. However, it does have the great advantage of grouping together the three actions performed on the loop-control variable, thus making it easier for the programmer to achieve correct loop control and for other people to understand his program. It is important to remember that the FOR statement provides leading decision loops.

We are now able to complete the description of the iteration element introduced in Section 2.7.3. The full element is shown in Figure 3.3. The initialisation and modification boxes are only used if the element is describing a counter-controlled loop; otherwise they are left blank.

Figure 3.3

Example 3.6

```
FOR NUM := 1 TO 10 DO
BEGIN
        CUBE := NUM**3;
        WRITELN (CUBE:3)
END;
```

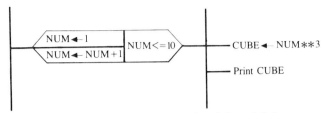

Examples 3.6 and 3.7 are identical to Examples 3.2 and 3.3 respectively, except that FOR statements have been used.

Example 3.7

```
READ (N);
FOR NUM := 1 TO N DO
BEGIN
        CUBE := NUM**3;
        WRITELN (CUBE:3)
END;
```

FOR NUM := 1 TO 10 DO

the modification is assumed to be +1. In the statement

FOR NUM := 10 DOWNTO 1 DO

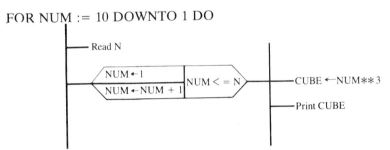

These two examples illustrate a number of noteworthy points.

First, the use of a FOR statement has resulted in a shorter sequence of code. In a large program with many FOR statements this could become a significant saving.

Second, the use of a counter-controlled iteration element has resulted in a corresponding reduction in the size of the structure diagram.

Third, the modification of the loop-control variable is not explicitly part of the FOR statement. In the statement
the modification is assumed to be −1. No other modifications are possible using the Pascal FOR statement. If a modification other than +1 or −1 is required, then the counter-controlled loop must be constructed from a WHILE statement. No such restriction applies to the counter-controlled iteration element in a structure diagram. For instance, it is quite possible

to make use of the element in Figure 3.4.

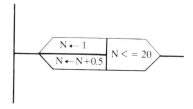

Figure 3.4

The equivalent of the Pascal FOR statement appears in many programming languages, and most of them do not share this same restriction.

Note that on exit from a FOR loop, the value of the loop-control variable is undefined. It cannot be assumed that it is one more (or one less) than the 'final' value specified in the FOR statement. Its value can of course be copied into another variable inside the FOR loop.

3.2.3 COBOL PERFORM statement

Leading decision loops are provided in COBOL by the PERFORM statement. This is a very powerful statement offering many variations; in this section we will restrict ourselves to some simple examples.

One obvious difference between COBOL and the majority of programming languages is that the body of a loop is stored *out-of-line* and not *in-line*. In other words, the loop control details appear in the main sequence of statements (that is, in-line) but the body of the loop is given an identifying name and located elsewhere in the program (that is, out-of-line). The effect is to organise program code in a succession of hierarchies or levels, the intention being to avoid cluttering up a particular level with coding which is logically from a different level of detail.

The following examples should be compared with the earlier Pascal versions.

Example 3.8

Print out the cubes of the numbers read from data, the end of the data being indicated by a value of zero.

```
ACCEPT NUM.
PERFORM PRINTCUBE UNTIL NUM = 0.
    .
    .
    .
    .
PRINTCUBE.
    COMPUTE CUBE = NUM ** 3.
    DISPLAY CUBE.
    ACCEPT NUM.
```

Note the use of the word UNTIL instead of WHILE. This has the effect of reversing the loop condition as compared with Pascal.

Example 3.9

Print out the cubes of the first N positive integers, where N is read from data.

```
ACCEPT N.
PERFORM PRINTCUBE VARYING NUM FROM 1 BY 1
                    UNTIL NUM > N.
    .
    .
    .
    .
PRINTCUBE.
    COMPUTE CUBE = NUM ** 3.
    DISPLAY CUBE.
```

There are two things to note about the somewhat cumbersome VARY-ING ... clause. First, it allows us to modify the loop-control variable by any amount we wish. Second, a complete condition follows the word UNTIL and not merely the final value of the loop-control variable.

Example 3.10

Print out the cubes of all positive integers, starting at 1, and stopping before the first cube which exceeds 100.

MOVE 1 TO CUBE.
PERFORM PRINTCUBE VARYING NUM FROM 2 BY 1
            UNTIL CUBE > 100.

.
.
.
.

PRINTCUBE.
        DISPLAY CUBE.
        COMPUTE CUBE = NUM ** 3.

The most important point to note about this example is that the loop-control variable does not need to appear in the loop condition. This gives the PERFORM statement great flexibility.

3.3 Trailing decision loops

So far, we have looked at iteration as a leading decision loop. Such decision loops are sufficient for the construction of any program, but some programming languages, Pascal included, offer a second type of loop. A flowchart for a *trailing decision loop* is given in Figure 3.5.

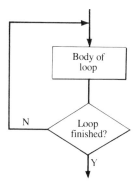

Figure 3.5

There is no equivalent structure diagram element.

   As can be seen, the decision trails behind the body of the loop, and hence the body of the loop must be executed at least once. Certainly, there are numerous instances where the programmer knows in advance that a loop must be executed at least once. However, it is always possible to fashion such a loop as a leading decision loop, and in general the provision of a trailing decision loop offers the programmer only marginal extra convenience.

The main objection to trailing decision loops is that they disperse the loop control over a potentially large span of program code. The loop condition is normally written at the end of the body of the loop. When reading a section of code and encountering the beginning of a trailing decision loop, the conditions under which the loop is repeated are not immediately obvious, especially if the body of the loop is large.

3.3.1 Pascal REPEAT statement

Pascal provides a trailing decision loop by means of the REPEAT... UNTIL statement. The body of the loop is delimited by the words REPEAT and UNTIL, so the normal delimiters BEGIN and END are not necessary. Indentation is, however, strongly recommended for the body of the loop in order to improve readability.

Example 3.11

Print out the cubes of all positive integers, starting at 1, and stopping before the first cube which exceeds 100.

```
NUM := 1;
CUBE := 1;
REPEAT
        WRITELN (CUBE:3);
        NUM := NUM+1;
        CUBE := NUM**3
UNTIL CUBE > 100;
```

Note that the loop condition is reversed from that used in the equivalent example employing WHILE.

Example 3.12

Print out the cubes of the numbers read from data, the end of the data being indicated by a value of zero.

```
READ (NUM);
REPEAT
        CUBE := NUM**3;
        WRITELN (CUBE:3);
        READ (NUM)
UNTIL NUM = 0;
```

Note that there must be at least one value in the data, before zero, for this section of coding to work correctly.

Example 3.13

Count the number of values in the data, the end of the data being indicated by a value of zero.

```
COUNT := 0;
READ (NUM);
REPEAT
        COUNT := COUNT+1;
        READ (NUM)
UNTIL NUM = 0;
```

Again, note that there must be at least one value in the data, before the terminating zero, for this section of coding to work correctly.

3.3.2 Trailing decision loops in COBOL

No single statement in COBOL provides a trailing decision loop mechanism. If use of a trailing decision loop in a COBOL program is required, the programmer must construct the loop from a combination of other statements.

Over the last few years, there has been a significant trend towards the use of structured programming in the construction of COBOL programs. The reason behind this trend will be discussed in a later chapter. Structured programming techniques tend to concentrate on the use of leading decision loops, and consequently the absence of a trailing decision loop mechanism in the COBOL language presents a programmer with no problems.

3.4 Nested loops

The body of a loop normally consists of several statements. Any one of these statements could itself be a looping statement. This *nesting* can be extended to create very complex control structures. Most languages do not specify the maximum number of levels that can be nested in this way. However, a limit is sometimes imposed by the compiler for the language. Different compilers may impose different limits for the same language. The imposing of limit normally has nothing to do with the language being compiled; it is invariably caused by the problems of writing a compiler and the approach to these problems adopted by the compiler-writer!

3.4.1 Nested loops in Pascal

In Pascal, the body of the loop is stored in-line immediately after the WHILE, FOR or REPEAT statement. One of the problems of nesting one loop inside the body of another loop is correctly identifying the statements that constitute the body of the inner loop. This problem is neatly solved in Pascal by the use of the BEGIN and END delimiters.

Figure 3.6 shows graphically the organisation of a simple nested loop structure.

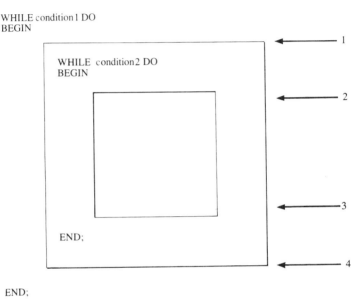

Figure 3.6

The body of the outer loop ranges from point 1 to point 4, and the body of the inner loop ranges from point 2 to point 3. Each execution of the body of the outer loop contains the complete repeated execution of the inner loop.

In a structure diagram using the notation introduced in Chapter 2, each additional level of nesting will simply cause the diagram to grow further to the right. If the structure diagram has been developed using stepwise refinement, each additional level of nesting may well be the subject of a separate structure diagram. In fact, it may be very difficult to draw a single structure diagram to describe a looping structure with several levels of nesting, simply because of the constraints of the piece of paper. There is some merit in the notion that structure diagrams should only ever be drawn on small pieces of paper, in order to force the programmer to break down the problem into its constituent parts!

The same problem applies to the Pascal code. As in Figure 3.6, indentation is used to help identify the ranges of the various levels of nesting. The indentation associated with deeply nested structures can push the coding inconveniently too far to the right. Fortunately, the same solution also applies. Providing that the body of a loop forms a coherent, logical segment of coding, which it will if the program has been designed correctly, it can be coded as a procedure or function and physically positioned elsewhere. The use of procedures and functions, with appropriately chosen names, can greatly improve the appearance and readability of deeply nested structures.

Example 3.14

Calculate the average number of goals scored by 10 soccer teams in their first 20 matches. The first 20 items of data relate to the first team, the next 20 items to the second team, and so on.

The structure of the data gives us the clue to the structure of the required program segment. Figure 3.7 shows the diagrammatic structure of the data. The first requirement is a loop, the body of which processes the data of a single team. To decide what needs to go into the body of this first loop, we consider the structure of the data for a single team. This is shown in diagrammatic form in Figure 3.8. It is clear that we need a second loop, the body of which processes the data for a single score. The second loop is nested within the first. A structure diagram for the complete solution is shown in Figure 3.9.

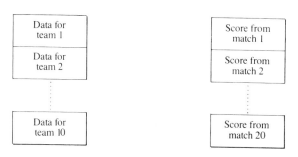

Figure 3.7   Figure 3.8

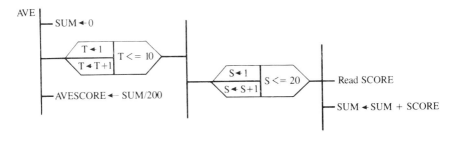

Figure 3.9

It is now an easy process to convert this into the necessary Pascal coding. Note that the outermost BEGIN and END pair is not strictly necessary since the body of the outer loop consists of a single statement: a FOR statement. It is included for consistency and readability.

```
SUM := 0;
FOR T := 1 TO 10 DO
BEGIN
      FOR S := 1 TO 20 DO
      BEGIN
            READ (SCORE);
            SUM := SUM+SCORE
      END
END;
AVESCORE := SUM/200;
```

Notice that this section of coding makes use of the constant values 10, 20 and 200. This is against good programming practice, which eliminates explicit constants from the body of a program. Instead, constants such as NOOFTEAMS and NOOFSCORES would be defined at the top of the program and used throughout. In this way, if the number of teams changed, for instance, only a single amendment would be needed.

Example 3.15

Read a file containing lines of text and count the number of occurrences of the letter 'E'.

Again we start by considering the structure of the data. It consists of a number of lines of text, and each line consists of a number of letters and spaces. This suggests a straightforward nested loop structure, as shown in Figure 3.10.

```
NOOFEES := 0;
WHILE NOT EOF DO
BEGIN
        WHILE NOT EOLN DO
        BEGIN
                READ (CH);
                IF CH = 'E' THEN
                        NOOFEES := NOOFEES+1
        END;
        READLN
END;
```

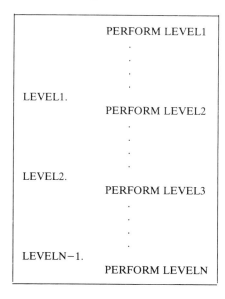

Figure 3.10

```
                        PERFORM LEVEL1
                            .
                            .
                            .
                            .
LEVEL1.
                        PERFORM LEVEL2
                            .
                            .
                            .
                            .
LEVEL2.
                        PERFORM LEVEL3
                            .
                            .
                            .
                            .
LEVELN-1.
                        PERFORM LEVELN
```

Figure 3.11

3.4.2 Nested loops in COBOL

Unlike Pascal, the body of the loop in COBOL is stored out-of-line in a separate paragraph. Each PERFORM statement in the body of a loop indicates an extra level of nesting and creates an additional paragraph to hold the body of the nested loop. Theoretically, any number of levels could be nested in this way, as shown in Figure 3.11.

The range of each level is clearly defined, and problems associated with repeated indentation do not arise. However, it is possible to inadvertently create a circular structure, as shown in Figure 3.12.

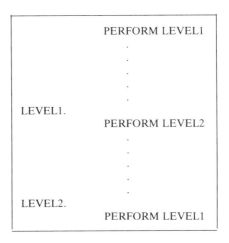

Figure 3.12

This is illegal COBOL, and the execution of a program containing such a structure is, at best, unpredictable. It might result accidentally when typing in the program, or it might be caused by a programmer modifying a program without first studying the structure diagram. It is impossible to create this circular structure in Pascal, without using procedures or functions, because the body of a nested loop is physically located within the body of the outer loop. Correspondingly, it is impossible to describe this circular structure with the structure diagram notation used in this book, without resorting to subdiagrams to establish the circularity.

Recursion is a programming technique which employs a circular control structure. Via its procedures and functions, Pascal explicitly supports recursion, whereas COBOL does not.

Example 3.16

Calculate the average number of goals scored by 10 soccer teams in their first 20 matches. The first 20 items of data relate to the first team, the next 20 items to the second team, and so on.

This is identical to Example 3.14. The analysis of the problem and the structure diagram are also identical.

```
        MOVE 0 TO SUM.
        PERFORM TEAM-LOOP  VARYING T FROM 1 BY 1
                           UNTIL T > 10.
        DIVIDE SUM BY 200 GIVING AVESCORE.
        .
        .
        .
        .
TEAM-LOOP
        PERFORM SCORE-LOOP VARYING S FROM 1 BY 1
                           UNTIL S > 20.
SCORE-LOOP.
        ACCEPT SCORE.
        ADD SCORE TO SUM.
```

As with the Pascal version of this coding, it would be possible to have a single loop with a control variable going from 1 to 200. It would be wrong to do so, however, since this program structure would not reflect the structure of the data. Documentation and later modification would be made harder.

The earlier comment about the elimination of explicit constants from the body of the program also applies here.

3.5 Nested selections

In Chapter 2, the control structure selection was introduced as one of the fundamental building blocks of program construction. A simple example of the use of a selection in a Pascal program was shown in Example 3.15. We now go on to look at more complicated uses of selection, involving *nested selection*.

An IF statement, either in Pascal or COBOL, is used to select one of two alternative courses of action. Consider the following section of coding.

```
IF condition   THEN   statement1
               ELSE   statement2
statement3
```

In the corresponding machine code, the following actions take place:

● Evaluate the condition
● If it is true, obey statement1
● If it is false, obey statement2
● Continue to obey the rest of the program, starting with statement3

When the ELSE part is not present, the third step is missing.

This simple two-way selection frequently occurs in programs. However, we are often faced with a more complicated selection where we need to choose one from several possibilities.

Example 3.17

From the numbers 1 . . . 7, print out the corresponding name from the list SLEEPY, HAPPY, DOPEY, GRUMPY, SNEEZY, BASHFUL and DOC.

A straightforward approach to this problem would be to use a series of seven consecutive IF statements.

Pascal:
```
IF DWARF = 1 THEN WRITE ('SLEEPY');
IF DWARF = 2 THEN WRITE ('HAPPY');
IF DWARF = 3 THEN WRITE ('DOPEY');
IF DWARF = 4 THEN WRITE ('GRUMPY');
IF DWARF = 5 THEN WRITE ('SNEEZY');
IF DWARF = 6 THEN WRITE ('BASHFUL');
IF DWARF = 7 THEN WRITE ('DOC');
```

COBOL:
```
IF DWARF = 1 DISPLAY 'SLEEPY'.
IF DWARF = 2 DISPLAY 'HAPPY'.
IF DWARF = 3 DISPLAY 'DOPEY'.
IF DWARF = 4 DISPLAY 'GRUMPY'.
IF DWARF = 5 DISPLAY 'SNEEZY'.
IF DWARF = 6 DISPLAY 'BASHFUL'.
IF DWARF = 7 DISPLAY 'DOC'.
```

This straightforward approach is in fact quite inefficient. The value of DWARF is always compared against all seven possible values. If on a particular occasion the value of DWARF is 4, the comparisons against 5, 6 and 7 are a complete waste of time. A better approach is to embed each successive IF statement within the ELSE part of the preceding IF statement. In this way we can be sure that a particular IF statement is executed only if all the previous conditions are false.

Pascal:
```
IF DWARF = 1 THEN WRITE ('SLEEPY')
ELSE IF DWARF = 2 THEN WRITE ('HAPPY')
ELSE IF DWARF = 3 THEN WRITE ('DOPEY')
ELSE IF DWARF = 4 THEN WRITE ('GRUMPY')
ELSE IF DWARF = 5 THEN WRITE ('SNEEZY')
ELSE IF DWARF = 6 THEN WRITE ('BASHFUL')
ELSE WRITE ('DOC');
```

COBOL:
```
IF DWARF = 1 DISPLAY 'SLEEPY'
ELSE IF DWARF = 2 DISPLAY 'HAPPY'
ELSE IF DWARF = 3 DISPLAY 'DOPEY'
ELSE IF DWARF = 4 DISPLAY 'GRUMPY'
ELSE IF DWARF = 5 DISPLAY 'SNEEZY'
ELSE IF DWARF = 6 DISPLAY 'BASHFUL'
ELSE DISPLAY 'DOC'.
```

Note that we have dispensed with the final IF statement and that any value of DWARF outside the range 1 to 6 will cause 'DOC' to be printed.

The structure diagram for this improved approach is shown in Figure 3.13.

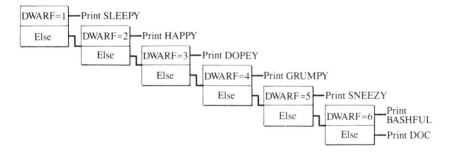

Figure 3.13

The level of nesting involved is much more apparent from the structure diagram than it is from the coding. However, the coding and the structure diagram both suffer from being long-winded and cumbersome. A much neater notation for the structure diagram is shown in Figure 3.14.

3.5.1 Pascal CASE statement

The type of nested selection shown in Example 3.17, which involves running down a list of possible values, is often called *cascade selection*. The Pascal CASE statement offers the programmer an alternative to nested IF statements, where the objective of the nested IF statements is cascade selection.

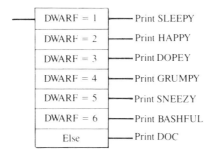

Figure 3.14

The CASE solution to Example 3.17 is shown in Figure 3.15.

```
CASE DWARF OF
    1 : WRITE   ('SLEEPY');
    2 : WRITE   ('HAPPY');
    3 : WRITE   ('DOPEY');
    4 : WRITE   ('GRUMPY');
    5 : WRITE   ('SNEEZY');
    6 : WRITE   ('BASHFUL');
    7 : WRITE   ('DOC')
END;
```

Figure 3.15

The CASE solution is obviously superior in terms of readability. However, the effect of a CASE statement is undefined if the value of the CASE variable (DWARF in Figure 3.15) is none of those listed. Some Pascal implementations appear to ignore the entire CASE statement if there is no match; other implementations give a run-time error. There is some discussion about the advisability of adding an ELSE clause to the CASE statement to deal with this problem. For the moment, it is common to embed the CASE statement inside an IF statement to ensure that the CASE is only executed if the variable does indeed contain one of the values listed. An example of this is shown in Figure 3.16.

COBOL has no equivalent to the CASE statement.

3.5.2 Complex nested selection

The simplest form of nested selection is the cascade selection, where the

```
IF (DWARF > = 1) AND (DWARF < = 7) THEN
   CASE DWARF OF
      1: WRITE   ('SLEEPY');
      2: WRITE   ('HAPPY');
      3: WRITE   ('DOPEY');
      4: WRITE   ('GRUMPY');
      5: WRITE   ('SNEEZY');
      6: WRITE   ('BASHFUL');
      7: WRITE   ('DOC')
   END;
```

Figure 3.16

nesting takes place only in the ELSE parts of the IF statements. This type of nested selection is fairly simple in concept, and easily understood by most programmers. However, there is no restriction on which statements can appear in the THEN part or the ELSE part of an IF statement. This gives great freedom for the construction of nested selection structures, including structures so complex that they are difficult to understand. Consider, for example, the following nested selection structure:

IF A = 1 THEN IF B = 2 THEN C: = 3 ELSE D: = 4;

Figure 3.17 shows two possible interpretations of this coding.

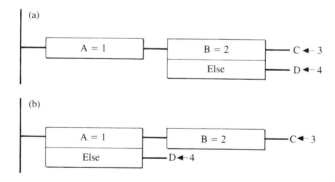

Figure 3.17

There is nothing in the statement to identify the IF to which the ELSE belongs. In fact, interpretation (a) is correct. The rule for matching an ELSE with its IF is as follows.

'Starting with the first ELSE from the beginning of a nested IF statement, an ELSE is paired with the closest unpaired IF. Continue towards the end of the nested IF until all the ELSEs have been paired.'

This rule applies to both Pascal and COBOL, and succeeds in removing the ambiguity of interpretation. However, it does not prevent programmers from meaning one thing and writing another. When indentation is misused the coding becomes even more confusing, as shown below:

```
IF A = 1
    THEN IF B = 2
            THEN C:=3
    ELSE D:=4;
```

The indentation makes no difference to the coding produced; the compiler will still come to interpretation (a). If interpretation (b) is actually intended, the Pascal programmer must use a BEGIN, END pair to delimit the range of the nested IF, as shown below:

```
IF A = 1 THEN
BEGIN
    IF B=2 THEN C:=3
END
ELSE D:=4;
```

The COBOL programmer faced with the same problem cannot resort to the useful delimiters BEGIN and END. Instead, he must create a dummy ELSE part so that the 'real' ELSE is paired with the correct IF. A section of COBOL coding corresponding to interpretation (b) is shown below:

```
IF A=1
    IF B=2 MOVE 3 TO C
    ELSE NEXT SENTENCE
ELSE MOVE 4 TO D.
```

The dummy ELSE NEXT SENTENCE is not always sufficient to solve the pairing problem in complex nested selection structures; it becomes necessary to adopt more elaborate coding techniques which only serve to reduce the readability of the program.

These relatively straightforward examples of nested selection are intended to indicate the problems of misinterpretation that can so easily arise. There is no virtue in creating complex structures of nested selection, however efficient the coding may be, when the result is unreadable and impossible to maintain. For this reason, it is quite common for an installation to adopt an in-house standard which bans all nested selection apart from cascade selection. The motto of a good programmer is 'keep it simple'.

3.6 Summary

This chapter has examined the way in which selection and iteration are expressed in the two languages Pascal and COBOL. Leading decision loops are particularly important to programmers who employ the techniques of structured programming, and the operation and application of such loops have been illustrated by numerous examples in the two languages. In order to clarify the differences between the various loop control features of Pascal, the chapter has also examined the use of a trailing decision loop. Such trailing decision loops are normally shunned by the advocates of structured programming, and they will not appear again throughout the remainder of this book.

An important programming practice described in this chapter is the use of nested control structures. Care must be taken to ensure that the benefits of compact coding, which can be achieved by nested structures, are not obscured by complex coding.

3.7 Exercise

Devise structure diagrams and write sections of Pascal and COBOL coding to solve the following problems:

● Multiply together the two numbers A and B to produce their product C, by using repeated addition.
● Divide TOP by BOTTOM to produce quotient QUOT and remainder REM by using repeated subtraction.
● Read in a character string, consisting of 0s and 1s and terminated by a ★, and output the length of the longest string of 1s.
● Read in a positive integer N and output the factorial of N.
● Read in a positive integer N and determine whether N is
  (a) prime
  (b) perfect.
● Read in three numbers A, B and C and output the largest.
● Read in an integer in the range 0–999 representing a number of pennies. Output the same value in terms of the number of one-pound coins, 50p coins, 20p coins, 10p coins, 5p coins, 2p coins and 1p coins, using the minumum number of coins.

CHAPTER 4

Simple data structures

4.1 Introduction □ 4.2 Fundamental classification of data □
4.3 Numeric data types □ 4.4 Non-numeric data types □ 4.5 Structured
data □ 4.6 Summary □ 4.7 Exercises

4.1 Introduction

Computers are designed for the storage, retrieval and transformation of data. The details of the transformation are embodied in a computer program, and it follows that languages must have the ability to describe the data on which programs operate. There are many different ways of classifying data, and this chapter introduces some of the simple kinds that are available on all computers and in the majority of languages.

Data types and data structures do not exist merely within programming languages. It is important to distinguish between the data structure itself and the way it is described in a particular language. This chapter discusses the characteristics of each data type and structure and then shows how they are represented in Pascal and COBOL. The operations commonly performed upon data types and structures are illustrated by numerous examples.

4.2 Fundamental classification of data

The word 'type' is often used in connection with the classification or description of data. Unfortunately, it has become associated with certain contexts, particularly Pascal, where it has a special meaning. In this book, the words 'type' and 'datatype' should be interpreted in their general sense. Where a specific Pascal context is to be assumed, the accompanying text will make this obvious.

Fundamentally, data may be classified into one of two types:

Numeric data, on which arithmetic operations may be performed; representing amounts of money, number of items in stock, distance between two points, voltages, etc.

Non-numeric data, on which sorting, searching and classification operations may be performed; representing names, addresses, switch settings, item codes, etc.

When designing a program, it is necessary to classify all the data in order to specify appropriate operations to manipulate the data. It clearly makes no sense to attempt to add together two items of data which are people's names, although it is not unknown for programmers to do so! In most programming languages, the statements which manipulate data are restricted to operating on a particular type of data. For instance, addition statements must operate on numeric data. Some statements can operate on different types of data, but even here compatibility between the operands involved is normally required. For instance, a 'copy' statement may be able to copy numeric to numeric, or non-numeric to non-numeric, but not a combination of the two. It is one of the functions of a compiler to check for compatibility between the operator and the operands.

In simple languages, such as BASIC, the programmer is restricted to one type of numeric data and one type of non-numeric data. For simple programs, this is sufficient. Indeed, it is theoretically sufficient for all programs, but only at the cost of considerable inconvenience and inefficiency during coding. This simple classification of data is inadequate for complex situations. Most programming languages allow the programmer to specify in much greater detail the attributes of each item of data.

4.3 Numeric data types

Numeric data items can be divided easily and obviously into two sub-categories: whole numbers and fractional numbers. Whole numbers are used to count discrete objects: the number of employees in a firm, the number of stages in a production line, and so on. The term *integer* is used to describe a data item having a whole number value. Fractional numbers are used to represent continuous values, the temperature in a furnace, the average of a list of numbers, and so on. The term *real* is used to describe a data item having a fractional value.

4.3.1 Integer numbers

Integers are positive or negative whole numbers. They are written as a sequence of consecutive digits, optionally preceded by a '+' or a '−' sign. In standard Pascal and COBOL, the digits must be decimal digits. In certain other languages, particularly low-level languages, it is possible to write integers in other bases.

COBOL defines the maximum size of an integer as 18 digits, irrespective of which computer is being used. Having a defined maximum size enforces a degree of standardisation and helps to make programs portable across different computers. It is also true to say that a number with 18 digits is a very large number, for example, 123456789987654321, and is more easily implemented on a large mainframe computer, for which COBOL was originally intended, than on a modern microcomputer.

Pascal does not define a maximum size for an integer and in theory an integer may be infinitely large. However, in practice, the limitations of computer hardware do impose an upper limit on the size of an integer. This limit is normally related to the computer's wordsize and will therefore vary from one computer to another. Pascal provides a constant identifier MAXINT whose value is the largest integer which can be held. The range of values of an integer variable is therefore

$$-\text{MAXINT}, \ldots, -2, -1, 0, 1, 2, \ldots, \text{MAXINT}$$

Typical values of MAXINT would be 32767 on a 16-bit computer and 2147483647 on a 32-bit computer. Both Pascal and COBOL have ways of restricting the range of an integer to values below the maximum allowed. In Pascal, the subrange facility allows the permitted range of an integer to be specified exactly. For example,

VAR
        DAYSINMONTH: 28..31;

defines an integer variable DAYSINMONTH with 4 possible correct values: 28, 29, 30 or 31. Any attempt to assign to DAYSINMONTH a value outside this range could be detected at run-time and reported to the programmer as a logic error. Clearly, this would be very useful during the debugging of a program. The use of subranges is to be encouraged.

In COBOL, it is not possible to specify the exact range of a variable, only the number of digits it contains. For instance, the declaration

01 DAYSINMONTH PIC 99.

defines a 2-digit integer variable capable of holding any integer 0 through 99. Even an attempt to assign to DAYSINMONTH a value outside this range will not normally give rise to a run-time failure. For instance, the statement

COMPUTE DAYSINMONTH = 10 * 10.

is likely to cause truncation rather than failure, that is, the two digits of DAYSINMONTH will become '00' and the '1' will be lost. COBOL at least forces the programmer to think about the range of possible values for a variable, but Pascal's mechanism for specifying the range is far superior.

4.3.2 Real numbers

Real numbers are positive or negative fractional numbers. In standard Pascal and COBOL, they are written as a sequence of decimal digits, including a single decimal point, and optionally preceded by a '+' sign or '−' sign. The following are examples of valid real numbers.

$$1.2345$$
$$-0.6$$
$$+1928.0$$

Apart from the conventional notation above, Pascal allows real numbers to be expressed in a *scientific notation*:

mantissa E exponent

The E should be read as 'times 10 to the power of'. Figure 4.1 shows examples of valid real numbers in this scientific notation, together with their equivalents in conventional form.

Scientific notation	Conventional notation
1.23E−10	0.000000000123
−6.9753E3	−6975.3
1E6	1000000
73.2E0	73.2

Figure 4.1

Just as with integer numbers, the computer hardware will impose limitations on the range and accuracy of real numbers stored in its memory. Conventionally, cither one or two memory words will be used to store each real number. This could amount to 16 bits for a microcomputer or 64 bits for a mainframe computer.

In order to accommodate numbers with both a whole number part and a fractional part, the *floating point* notation is used. This is similar to Pascal's scientific notation, the number being stored in two parts: the mantissa and the exponent, but the number being stored in base 2 and not base 10. The range and precision of a stored real number depend on the allocation of bits between the exponent and the mantissa.

The greater the number of bits allocated to the exponent, the greater is the range of the numbers that can be stored. If 8 bits are allocated, for example, the exponent can have any value between -128 and $+127$ and the mantissa can be scaled by any factor between

$$2^{-128} \text{ and } 2^{+127}$$

The greater the number of bits allocated to the mantissa, the higher is the precision of numbers that can be stored. If 24 bits were allocated, for example, the mantissa could have any value in the range

$$-8388608 \text{ to } +8388607$$

In decimal terms, this means that any number with 6 significant figures (but not necessarily with 7) could be represented exactly. The largest mantissa in common use on large mainframe computers can hold numbers exactly with up to 17 significant decimal digits.

It is clear that the hardware designer has to trade precision with range when deciding on the floating point format for real numbers. The more bits allocated to the mantissa, the fewer available for the exponent, and vice versa. The floating point format varies from one computer to another, and thus the range and precision of real numbers may also vary between different implementations of the same language. You should consult the language manuals for your computer to discover its limitations. As a rough guide, the larger the computer the larger the range and precision of real numbers.

In theory at least, real numbers represent infinitely variable values. There is, therefore, no 'real' equivalent to the subrange facility offered by Pascal for the declaration of integers. In Pascal, a real variable is simply declared as REAL, and a standard number of bits is allocated for its storage. For example, the declaration of three variables is shown below.

```
VAR
        LENGTH,
        HEIGHT,
        WIDTH  :  REAL;
```

For Pascal implemented on a large mainframe computer, real numbers have, typically, a range of $10^{\pm70}$ and a precision of 6 significant decimal digits.

In COBOL, the notation used for declaring integers is extended to cope with real numbers. For instance,

01 WIDTH PIC 9(4) V99.

defines a real variable called WIDTH with 4 digits before the decimal point and 2 after. If a value which does not conform to this format is assigned to WIDTH, then truncation will take place at one or both ends. For example, the statement

COMPUTE WIDTH = 10 * 1234.5678

obviously produces a true value of

12345.678

but causes WIDTH to be assigned the value

2345.67

This truncation would not normally be reported as a run-time error; the programmer must take it into account when he defines the size of a variable.

The maximum number of digits that can be specified in a COBOL PICTURE clause is 18. In this way, any real number between

V9(18)   and   9(18)V

can be defined. This corresponds approximately to the number of significant digits that can be held in the floating point format on a large computer. However, the range is far smaller than the range available in floating point format. This is the position with standard COBOL.

Some non-standard versions of COBOL allow the programmer to take full advantage of the range of floating point numbers. This is done via an extension to the USAGE clause. Consider, for example, the following declarations:

01   WIDTH   USAGE   IS   COMP−1.
01   HEIGHT   USAGE   IS   COMP−2.

This defines WIDTH as a single precision floating point variable (normally about 6 significant digits) and HEIGHT as a double precision floating point variable (normally about 17 significant figures). In both cases, however, the available range is enormous (typically from 10^{-70} to 10^{+70}). At the expense of loss in precision, the programmer can thus manipulate very large, or very small, numbers. The fact that this feature is non-standard, and that there is a consequent reduction in the ease of maintenance of programs employing it, should not be forgotten.

4.3.3 Accuracy in integer arithmetic

In Pascal, the range of an integer value is defined by MAXINT. In COBOL, it is defined as 18 digits. Provided that an integer value is within the appropriate range, it can be stored exactly, that is, there is no *representational error*.

As we have seen, both Pascal and COBOL allow the range of a particular integer variable to be defined as less than the range offered by the computer hardware. If the value of a variable goes outside its particular range, Pascal responds with a run-time error message and COBOL responds with truncation. If integer arithmetic generates a value which is outside the maximum range for the computer, then the hardware generates a run-time error and stops the program. This is called *arithmetic overflow*.

Overflow can be caused by the result of a computation being too large, in a positive or negative sense, to be held in the computer's integer notation. Overflow can also be caused by an intermediate value, produced during the evaluation of an expression, being too large. For example, if X, Y and Z are integers with values near the maximum value, then the evaluation of the expression

$$X*Y/Z$$

is likely to cause an overflow at the point that X is multiplied by Y, even though the value of the complete expression may be well within range. It is interesting to note that evaluation of the equivalent expression

$$X/Z*Y$$

is unlikely to cause an overflow. When dealing with integers near the maximum possible value, a programmer must consider the order of evaluation.

4.3.4 Accuracy in real arithmetic

The representation and manipulation of real numbers by a computer is inherently inaccurate. In order to investigate some of the problems which arise with real numbers, let us consider a decimal computer which stores real numbers as a signed one-digit exponent and a signed three-digit mantissa. The decimal point is assumed to be immediately to the left of the first digit in the mantissa.

| +9 | +999 | Largest positive number, | $+.999 \times 10^9$ |

| +9 | −999 | Largest negative number, | $-.999 \times 10^9$ |

| −9 | +001 | Smallest positive number, | $+.001 \times 10^{-9}$ |

| −9 | −001 | Smallest negative number, | $-.001 \times 10^{-9}$ |

Figure 4.2, which is not drawn to scale, shows the numbers which can be represented by this notation.

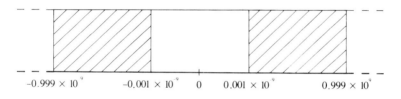

-0.999×10^9	-0.001×10^9	0	0.001×10^9	0.999×10^9

Figure 4.2

As can be seen, the notation cannot represent numbers which are very close to zero. Conventionally, zero itself is represented by a zero exponent and zero mantissa:

| 0 | 000 |

Clearly, arithmetic overflow is just as much a problem with real numbers as it is with integers, and the same comments and warnings apply. However, real arithmetic is also beset by *arithmetic underflow*, where values are so close to zero that they cannot be represented. Consider multiplying the smallest positive number by itself.

$$
\begin{array}{r}
0.001 \times 10^{-9} \\
\times \quad 0.001 \times 10^{-9} \\
\hline
0.000001 \times 10^{-18} \qquad = 0.001 \times 10^{-21}
\end{array}
$$

This result is far too small to be represented by our notation. When such underflow occurs, it is detected by hardware and, on most computers, the result is set to zero as the best approximation to the true answer.

Another problem which can occur with real arithmetic is called *loss of significance*. This happens when real numbers of widely different magnitude are added or subtracted. In floating point addition or subtraction, it is necessary to make the exponents of the two numbers equal before the operation takes place. Normally, the number with the smaller exponent is adjusted. Consider the following example:

$$0.990 \times 10^6 + 0.293 \times 10^4 - 0.990 \times 10^6$$

The answer should be 0.293×10^4.

We first perform the addition by adjusting the number with the smaller exponent, to obtain

$$
\begin{array}{r}
0.990 \times 10^6 \\
+0.002 \times 10^6 \\
\hline
0.992 \times 10^6
\end{array}
$$

This result is clearly inaccurate. If we now perform the subtraction, we obtain

$$
\begin{array}{r}
0.992 \times 10^6 \\
-0.990 \times 10^6 \\
\hline
0.002 \times 10^6 \qquad = 0.200 \times 10^4
\end{array}
$$

instead of the true answer 0.293×10^4. This error results from the fact that only a fixed number of significant digits can be held. Even if rounding instead of truncation were used during the equalisation of the exponents, the result would still be inaccurate.

In digital computers, real numbers are held in binary and not in decimal. However, the problems associated with decimal floating point arithmetic apply equally well to binary floating point arithmetic. Moreover, our familiarity with the decimal notation may make us ignore (at our peril) problems of representation in the binary notation. For example, the number 0.3 can be represented exactly as a decimal fraction but has no exact binary equivalent. When we use such numbers in our source programs, we must remember that the object program contains only approximations to them.

For all the above reasons, programmers need to take great care when performing arithmetic on real numbers. A related situation which commonly gives rise to problems is where real numbers are compared with each other for equality. Representational and computational errors may give rise to slight inaccuracies in the numbers stored, and numbers which should have been equal are found to be different. The standard technique is to avoid comparing two real numbers directly and to compare instead their difference with a small constant. If their difference is less than this constant they are assumed to be equal. For example, given that X and Y are real variables, instead of writing

$$\text{IF } X = Y \ldots$$

we write

$$\text{IF ABS } (X - Y) < 0.0000001 \ldots$$

4.4 Non-numeric data types

In most programming languages, non-numeric data means character, or character strings, and Boolean values.

Not all languages, however, offer both these types of non-numeric data and the operations allowed vary considerably from one language to another. For instance, Boolean variables are not available in standard BASIC. COBOL offers a form of Boolean variable but restricts the ways it may be referenced.

Some languages, Pascal in particular, offer the programmer facilities for defining his own types of non-numeric data. Indeed, it could be argued that the SUBRANGE mechanism allows the Pascal programmer to define his own types of numeric data.

In this chapter, we will restrict our attention to characters and Boolean values.

4.4.1 Characters

The user of a computer communicates with a system by keying in characters on a keyboard. The system communicates with a user by displaying characters on a VDU screen. On some recent systems, this character-based dialogue has been replaced by a dialogue based on icons (graphic pictures from which the user selects in order to indicate his intentions), but this tends to be aimed primarily at inexperienced or non-specialist users. Character-based dialogues are still the common basis of the man–machine interface for computer professionals.

The characters which are recognised by the computer form the computer's character set. A character keyed on a VDU keyboard is converted into a unique binary pattern which is recognised by the rest of the system as representing that particular character. Unfortunately, the association between a character and a bit pattern is not standardised across all

computers. The two most common character codes are EBCDIC, which uses an 8-bit pattern to represent each character, and ASCII, which uses a 7-bit pattern. Neither code uses all the available bit patterns.

Examples of characters are

'A' 'b' '1' '0' '+' '?' '.' ' '

The last example is the blank, or space, character. The quotes are needed to distinguish between characters and other items in a language. For instance 'X' is a character but X may be the name of a variable.

When the character set is sorted in ascending order of the corresponding binary patterns, it forms the *collating sequence* of the computer. Although this sequence varies from one machine to another, 'A' is always less than 'B', 'B' is always less than 'C', and so on. In addition, '0' is less than '1', '1' is less than '2', and so on. There is, however, no standardisation on whether 'A' is less than '1', or '1' is less than 'A'. The positions in the collating sequence of special characters such as '+' and '?' vary from one computer to another.

In Pascal, character variables are defined as type CHAR, as in the example below.

VAR
        CODE,
        CH : CHAR;

Pascal also provides two standard functions, ORD and CHR, which make it easy to convert a character into the corresponding character code, and back again. Assume that BINPAT is declared as an integer and that the character variable CODE has the value 'X'. The statement

BINPAT := ORD(CODE) ;

puts into BINPAT the decimal equivalent of the binary pattern associated with the character 'X'. The subsequent statement

CH : = CHR(BINPAT);

would put into CH the character whose code is in BINPAT, that is, the character 'X'. These standard functions make it easy for the Pascal programmer to print out the collating sequence; see Exercise 4.10.

In COBOL, all variables are assumed to hold their values as characters, the DISPLAY format, unless the programmer specifies otherwise. For example, the variable

01 NUM PIC 999.

would hold the value 123 as three separate characters: '1', '2' and '3'. Before any arithmetic can be performed on this variable, it must be converted into a true binary number. This conversion is performed invisibly to the programmer by code generated by the compiler. However, the programmer should be aware of the need for this conversion because of the increased run-time it causes. It is clearly unwise to hold a number as a character string if it is heavily involved in arithmetic. In such circumstances, the programmer should specify the COMPUTATIONAL format to ensure that the number is stored in binary.

COBOL was designed specifically to be good at character manipulation, and character data is designated as either NUMERIC, ALPHABETIC or ALPHANUMERIC. Character variables may be tested explicitly to determine to which subtype they belong, as shown in the following examples.

IF NUM IS NOT NUMERIC ...
IF NAME IS ALPHABETIC ...

This facility is very useful during data vetting. Most languages, including Pascal, are less adept at character handling and usually do not subdivide the character classification.

The term *character string* is used to describe a sequence of characters which are collectively considered and manipulated as a single item. In COBOL, any character variable of length greater than one can be considered to be a character string. For example, the following declarations all define character strings, although they are from different subtypes.

```
01   NAME       PIC  A (20).
01   TAXCODE    PIC  999.
01   ITEMCODE   PIC  X (6).
```

Attempting to access substrings within these character strings is possible, but inconvenient.

In Pascal, however, a character variable can only hold a single character. To store a character string, Pascal resorts to a one-dimensional array of character variables. This will be discussed in more detail in Section 4.5.1. Attempting to access substrings is again possible, but inconvenient.

The number of operations specifically designed to support character handling varies from one language to another, and depends on the design objectives of the language. It is not surprising that COBOL offers good facilities for data vetting, for sorting character strings, for searching tables of character strings, for scanning a character string for a substring, and so on. Some of these facilities will be described further in Section 4.5. Pascal, on the other hand, has more general-purpose objectives and its character handling facilities are not so well developed.

4.4.2 Booleans

Practically all programming languages make use of Boolean expressions to decide between alternative courses of action. We have already seen how both Pascal and COBOL use conditions in their selection and iteration structures. Not all languages, however, offer genuine Boolean variables. We shall see that Pascal is one such language and that COBOL offers only a restricted form of Boolean variable.

Boolean variables derive their name from George Boole, an English mathematician who invented a system of logic using only two values: 'true' and 'false'. In a computer programming language, Boolean variables are used to describe relationships between other variables in the program. Most programming languages, including Pascal and COBOL, do not allow Boolean values to be input as data.

It is always possible to write a program without using Boolean variables, and in this sense they are an optional feature within a language. Many programmers fail to make appropriate use of Boolean variables, simply because they are more practised in the handling of other types of variables. This is a pity since Boolean variables used properly can considerably improve the readability of a program, and hence facilitate its maintenance.

In Pascal, Boolean variables are declared in the same way as any other type, as shown below.

```
VAR
        ERRORSFOUND,
        DUNENOUGH        : BOOLEAN;
```

The two variables EOF (end of file) and EOLN (end of line) are Boolean variables provided automatically by Pascal. Also provided are the constants TRUE and FALSE. Boolean variables may be used anywhere that a Boolean expression may be used. Additionally, a Boolean variable may be the subject of an assignment statement, as shown below:

```
ERRORSFOUND := FALSE;
DUNENOUGH := X < Y; (where X and Y are numeric variables)
```

The closest that COBOL comes to providing Boolean variables is by its level-88 condition-names, an example of which is shown below.

```
01   ITEMNUM PIC 999.
     88   VALID-ITEMNUM VALUE 0 THRU 99, 990.
```

Condition-names are attached to ordinary data-names. In the above example, VALID-ITEMNUM is 'true' if the value of ITEMNUM is 990 or less than 100, and 'false' if ITEMNUM has any other value. Condition-names are intended primarily to facilitate data vetting. COBOL provides no equivalent to Pascal's constants TRUE and FALSE. The only way to change the value of a condition-name is to change the value of the data-name with which it is associated.

Both Pascal and COBOL offer the logical operators AND, OR and NOT for use with Boolean variables/condition-names.

It is important that all variables in any program be assigned names which represent their function, but it is particularly important for Boolean variables and condition-names. The enhanced readability of

IF NOT VALID-ITEMNUM PERFORM ERRORMESS.

compared to that of the possible alternative

IF ITEMNUM > 99 AND < 990
        OR > 990 PERFORM ERRORMESS.

is at least partly due to the sensible choice of a name for the condition-name.

4.5 Structured data

The data types we have looked at so far, integers, reals, characters and Booleans, could be considered to be the primitive, lowest-level types of data. Frequently, we need to consider a collection of such primitive items of data which have been organised in some way. Such a collection of data items is called a *data structure*. A data structure may be a collection of items of the same type, such as a list of people's names, or it may be a collection of items of various types, such as an entry in a parts list, containing a part's name, code number, number in stock and unit price.

In this chapter, we will look at some simple data structures containing items all of the same type. Chapter 7 will deal with more complex data structures.

4.5.1 Vectors

A *vector* is a group of elements given a common name. Each element is of the same type, and an individual element is identified by means of its position within the group. Position within the group is specified by means of a subscript, enclosed in brackets, following the group name. Figure 4.3 shows a vector called DISC with three elements.

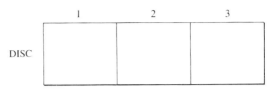

Figure 4.3

The first element is identified as DISC [1], the second element as DISC [2] and the third element as DISC [3]. The subscript does not have to be a constant; it could be a variable or even an expression. In fact, the greatest advantages are to be gained when the value of the subscript can be varied as a program executes. Consider the following example.

Example 4.1

Calculate the discounted cost DCOST to a client of ordering NUM articles at a cost of UNITCOST each. Clients belong to either discount group 1, discount group 2 or discount group 3, as indicated by the value of CLIENTGROUP, and attract a discount as follows:

Discount group 1 : 30%
Discount group 2 : 22%
Discount group 3 : 15%

A simple but tedious approach, in Pascal, might be as follows:

```
DCOST := NUM * UNITCOST;
IF CLIENTGROUP = 1 THEN
    DCOST := DCOST * 0.7
ELSE IF CLIENTGROUP = 2 THEN
    DCOST := DCOST * 0.78
ELSE DCOST := DCOST * 0.85;
```

This could perhaps be improved by the use of a CASE statement, but the best solution involves using a vector of discount rates, such as shown in Figure 4.4.

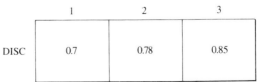

Figure 4.4

The coding then reduces to

DCOST : = NUM ∗ UNITCOST ∗ DISC [CLIENTGROUP];

In Pascal, the vector of discount rates would be declared as below

VAR
        DISC : ARRAY [1 . . 3] OF REAL;

Before any discounted costs are calculated, the elements of DISC would
have to be given their values by means of

$$
\begin{aligned}
&\text{DISC } [1] := 0.7;\\
&\text{DISC } [2] := 0.78;\\
&\text{DISC } [3] := 0.85;
\end{aligned}
$$

Example 4.1 is in fact a very simple example of the definition and use of
ARRAY type variables in Pascal. The language Pascal offers quite flexible
and powerful facilities for processing vectors. For example, the elements
of a vector can be of any type available in Pascal: INTEGER, REAL,
BOOLEAN, CHAR, ARRAY and others we have not yet mentioned.
Also, a subscript does not have to be a constant or simple variable; any
expression can be used. For example, the world population for each year
this century could be recorded in the vector defined below:

VAR
        WORLDPOP : ARRAY [1900 . .1999] OF 0 . . MAXINT;

More significantly, subscripts do not need to be numeric. In simple terms,
the only restriction on the possible values for a subscript is that they are
finite in number and arranged in a recognised sequence. For example, the
following vector:

VAR
        LETTERCOUNT : ARRAY ['A' . . 'Z'] OF 0 . . MAXINT;

could be used to count the occurrences of the letters of the alphabet.
Assuming the type definition

TYPE
    MONTHNAME = (JAN,FEB,MAR,APR,MAY,JUN,JUL,AUG,
                                SEP,OCT,NOV,DEC);

the following vector

```
VAR
        DAYSINMONTH : ARRAY [MONTHNAME] OF 28 .. 31;
```

could be used to hold the number of days in each month.

In COBOL, on the other hand, subscripts must be of type integer and the first element of a vector is always accessed by a subscript value of 1. The OCCURS clause is used to define a vector, as shown in the following example:

```
01   WHOLETHING.
        03    DAYSINMONTH PIC 99 OCCURS 12 TIMES.
```

The word TIMES is optional. An individual element is again selected by means of a subscript, this time in round brackets, as in the following examples.

```
DAYSINMONTH (2)
DAYSINMONTH (MONTHNUM)
```

A subscript must be either an integer numeric literal or an integer variable; arithmetic expressions are not allowed. A very useful facility provided by COBOL is the ability to refer to the entire vector as a single item. For example, assuming the following definition

```
01   TALLEYS.
        03    LETTERCOUNT PIC 99 OCCURS 26.
```

all the counts could be set to zero by the single instruction

```
MOVE ZERO TO TALLEYS.
```

In COBOL, an OCCURS clause may be attached to a group item, as shown below:

```
01   CODE-LIST.
        03    ITEM-CODE OCCURS 3.
                05    ALPH PIC A.
                05    NUM PIC 999.
```

Figure 4.5 shows this data structure in diagrammatic form.

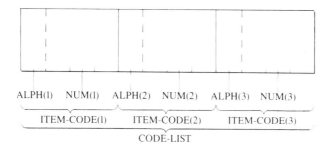

Figure 4.5

All the elements of replication are identical, but each element can be internally divided into subelements which can be individually referenced. This feature of COBOL makes it possible to describe very complex data structures.

4.5.2 Multi-dimensional arrays

Vectors are, in fact, *one-dimensional arrays* and both Pascal and COBOL support the definition of arrays with more than one dimension. If each element of a vector is itself a vector, then the entire data structure is a *two-dimensional array*. A two-dimensional array can be thought of as a table, having rows and columns. If each element of a two-dimensional array is itself a vector, then the entire data structure is a *three-dimensional array*. Books on COBOL tend to use the word 'table' to describe all arrays, regardless of the number of dimensions, mainly in an attempt to avoid technical jargon. Figure 4.6 shows examples of one-, two- and three-dimensional arrays.

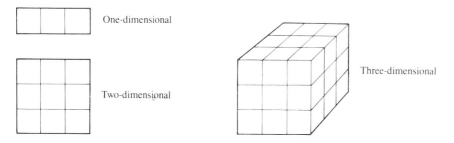

Figure 4.6

Pascal specifies no limit on the number of dimensions, but a particular implementation of Pascal may impose its own limit. The maximum number of dimensions in COBOL is three which is more than adequate for the types of problem programmed in COBOL. In fact, for all programming languages, the vast majority of programs will not require arrays with more than one or two dimensions.

In order to define a two-dimensional array, Pascal and COBOL simply extend the notations they employ for vectors. For instance, the following Pascal coding defines a table with 4 rows and 3 columns.

VAR
        DISCTAB : ARRAY [1 . . 4,1 . . 3] OF REAL;

Allowing certain assumptions about the size of each element, the equivalent definition in COBOL is shown below:

01   FILLER.
       03 FILLER OCCURS 4.
       05 DISCTAB OCCURS 3 PIC 99V99.

In order to access an individual element in a two-dimensional array, two subscripts are necessary: the first subscript indicates the row and the second subscript indicates the column. Figure 4.7 shows the DISCTAB table defined above. The element marked * is referred to as

            DISCTAB [3,2] in Pascal
    and   DISCTAB (3,2) in COBOL

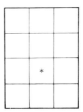

Figure 4.7

The extension to three dimensions is straightforward. Figure 4.8 shows a structure with three 'slices', each slice being a table of four rows and two columns.

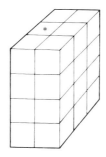

Figure 4.8

A possible definition of this structure in Pascal is shown below:

VAR
        CUBOID : ARRAY [1..4,1..2,1..3] OF INTEGER;

In COBOL, the same structure could be defined by

```
01  FILLER.
    03   FILLER OCCURS 4.
        05   FILLER OCCURS 2.
            07   CUBOID OCCURS 3 PIC 9(4).
```

The element marked * is referenced as

                CUBOID [1,1,2] in Pascal
      and   CUBOID (1,1,2) in COBOL

The ability in COBOL to attach an OCCURS clause to a group item sometimes makes it difficult to determine exactly how many dimensions a structure has. Consider the following example:

```
01  FILLER.
    03   R OCCURS 3.
        05   P PIC X.
        05   Q OCCURS 3 PIC 9.
```

Elements named R and P must be accessed with one subscript and elements named Q must be accessed with two subscripts. Is the structure one-dimensional or two-dimensional?

4.5.3 Operations on arrays

In Example 4.1, a one-dimensional array was used to hold discount rates. A particular element was identified and accessed directly in order to extract a required discount rate. In general, it is more common for many, if not all, of the elements of an array to be accessed and the same operation to be performed upon them. For instance, it is frequently necessary to initialise all the elements of an array to zero, or to fill the elements of an array with items read from data. It is quite natural to perform this type of array operation by means of a loop. Consider the following Pascal definition:

```
VAR
      LETTERCOUNT : ARRAY ['A' .. 'Z'] OF 0 .. MAXINT;
```

To initialise the elements to zero, the following coding could be used, assuming that CH has been defined as a variable of type CHAR:

```
FOR CH := 'A' TO 'Z' DO
      ARRAY [CH] := 0;
```

Now consider the following definition of a one-dimensional array in COBOL:

```
01   WHOLETHING.
      03   ITEM PIC 99 OCCURS 10.
```

Assuming suitable definitions for SUMMER and SUB, the following coding finds the sum of the elements of WHOLETHING:

```
            MOVE 0 TO SUMMER.
            PERFORM ADDITUP VARYING SUB FROM 1 BY 1
                  UNTIL SUB > 10.
            .
            .
            .
            .
ADDITUP.
            ADD ITEM (SUB) TO SUMMER.
```

In both these examples, the same operation is to be performed on all the elements of the arrays; the Pascal FOR statement, and the COBOL equivalent, are the natural choices for looping statement. In other cases, it will not be known in advance how many of the array elements need to be processed, and it may be more appropriate to use Pascal's WHILE statement, or its equivalent.

When an element-by-element access to a multi-dimensional array needs to be performed, the most appropriate control structure is a nested loop. Consider the following Pascal definition of a two-dimensional array:

VAR
        TABLE : ARRAY [1 . . 10,1 . . 20] OF INTEGER;

To fill this array with numbers read from an input file, the following nested loop could be used:

FOR I := 1 TO 10 DO
        FOR J := 1 TO 20 DO
                READ (TABLE [I,J]);

Study the coding and satisfy yourself that the elements are filled in the order

TABLE [1,1], TABLE [1,2], . . ., TABLE [1,10], TABLE [2,1],
TABLE [2,2], . . .

The array is filled row by row, and not column by column. This is the effect of having the outer loop control the first subscript, and is the conventional way of scanning an array in both Pascal and COBOL.

Three operations which are frequently performed on one-dimensional arrays are *searching*, *sorting* and *merging*. These three operations have been the subjects of many books, and will not be treated in any detail here. However, all programmers should be aware of the correct approach to these operations; and a brief introduction will be included.

Searching involves systematically examining the elements of an array, looking for a specific value or for an element which satisfies a particular condition. The actual method of searching employed depends on the way in which the values are stored in the array. Let us suppose that there is no rationale behind the way in which the values are stored, that is, they are in random order. In such circumstances, we may as well start at the beginning of the array and examine each element in turn until we find the one we are seeking or discover that it is not in the array. This is called a *linear search*.

Example 4.2

Design a program to perform a lincar seach of a one-dimensional array NAMES of length LEN, looking for an element with the same value as WANTED. If the search is successful output 'FOUNDIT', otherwise output

'NOTFOUNDIT'.

The program must examine NAMES [1], NAMES [2], . . . and so on, until one of two conditions becomes true: either WANTED is found, or the entire array has been examined without success. Figure 4.9 shows an outline structure diagram which seems appropriate.

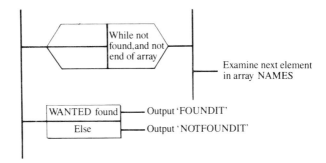

Figure 4.9

The variable POS can be used as a subscript. Provided that POS does not exceed N, the array is not exhausted. A Boolean variable FOUND can also be used to indicate whether the search has been successful. The next refinement of the structure diagram is shown in Figure 4.10.

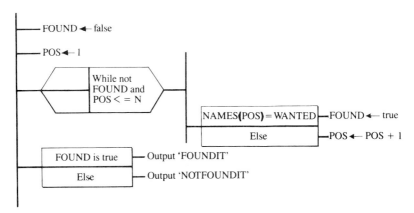

Figure 4.10

Note that at the end of this program segment, POS contains the subscript value of the element containing WANTED. The conversion of this program design into either Pascal or COBOL is left as an exercise.

Now suppose that the values in the array are stored in order. We can take advantage of this ordering in the design of the search. If the middle element is examined, it can be determined whether the value being sought is in the upper or lower half. This process is continued for the remainder of the array until the wanted element is found or it is decided that it is not present. At each stage the remainder of the array is halved. Consequently, this approach is called a *binary search*.

Example 4.3

Design a program to perform a binary search of a one-dimensional array NAMES of length N, looking for an element with the same value as WANTED. The elements of NAMES are stored in ascending order. If the search is successful output 'FOUNDIT', otherwise output 'NOTFOUNDIT'.

An outline structure diagram is shown in Figure 4.11.

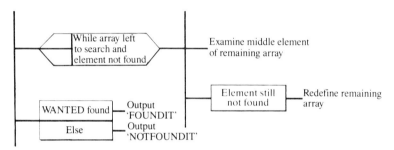

Figure 4.11

Two pointers can be used, FIRST and LAST, to identify the bounds of the remaining array, and a third pointer MIDDLE to identify the middle element. Obviously, when the remaining array has an even number of elements, there is no unique middle element; but it does not matter whether the first or the second of the two candidates is chosen. Figure 4.12 shows the next refinement of the structure diagram.

The binary search algorithm is more complex than that of a linear search, and it can only be used where the array is ordered. However, it is also much faster, and becomes increasingly attractive as the size of the array increases.

Sorting involves rearranging the elements of an array into a particular order. There are many different techniques for sorting; each has its own strengths and weaknesses and particular circumstances in which it is suitable. We will consider one simple method of sorting.

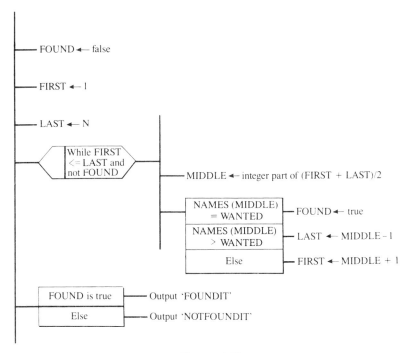

Figure 4.12

Example 4.4

Design a program to sort an array **NAMES** of N elements into ascending order.

It does not matter whether the individual elements are numbers or character strings. First, the entire array is examined to find the smallest element, which is then exchanged with the element at the beginning of the array. The first element can now be ignored and the process repeated with the remainder of the array, starting at the second element. The entire array is sorted by continuing in this fashion. An outline structure diagram for this is given in Figure 4.13.

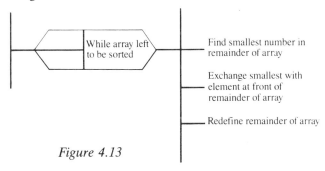

Figure 4.13

A number of variables can be used: FRONT, to point to the beginning of the remainder of the array; REST, to scan the remainder of the array; SVAL, to hold the value of the smallest element; and SPOINT, to hold the position of the smallest element. The refined structure diagram is given in Figure 4.14.

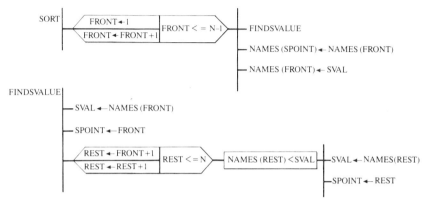

Figure 4.14

This solution is not necessarily optimal. For instance, in its present form it is possible for an element to be 'exchanged' with itself if the smallest element is already at the front of the array. However, putting a test in to avoid this may not produce an overall improvement in speed.

Merging involves combining two arrays which are ordered in some fashion to produce a third array. The third array contains the elements of the first two arrays and is ordered in the same fashion. Once again, a simple example will be considered in order to illustrate the principles involved.

Example 4.5

Design a program to merge together two arrays NAMES1 and NAMES2, of lengths N1 and N2 respectively, to produce a third array NAMES3. The elements of NAMES1 and NAMES2 are stored in ascending order.

The first step is to decide how to treat values which are common to both arrays. Should they both be transferred to the third array, or should only one be transferred and the other discarded? In practice, the answer will be obvious from the circumstances. Let us adopt the second alternative.

The general approach will be as follows. Start by comparing the elements at the beginning of the two arrays. If they are the same, copy one to the new array and discard the other. If they are different, simply copy the smaller to the new array. Repeat this process until one of the arrays is exhausted. Then copy the remainder of the other array to the new array. An outline structure diagram for this process is given in Figure 4.15.

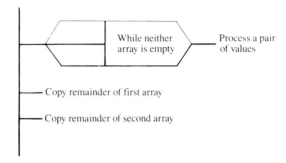

Figure 4.15

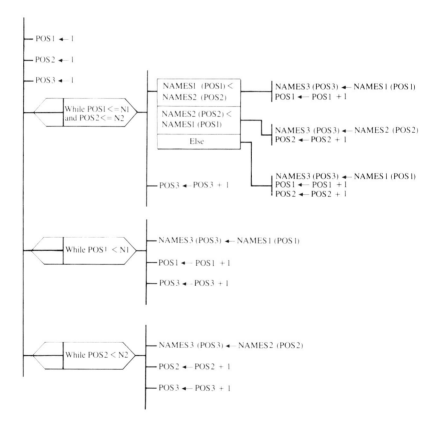

Figure 4.16

'Copy remainder of first array', for example, has no effect if the first array is already exhausted. The three variables POS1, POS2 and POS3 must be used to indicate the position reached in the three arrays. The refined structure diagram is shown in Figure 4.16.

4.6 Summary

In this chapter we have examined some of the simple data types and data structures and shown how they are represented in Pascal and COBOL. Moreover, the operations commonly performed on these data types and structures have been illustrated by sequences of coding. The important point, however, is that data types and structures can be studied independently of any programming language. The classification of data by type and structure is fundamental to all information processing. Only by understanding these abstract concepts can a programmer properly handle data in his programs.

The contents of this chapter form the basis of the study of more advanced data structures in Chapter 7.

4.7 Exercises

4.7.1   Write a small Pascal program to discover the value of MAXINT on your system.

4.7.2   Write a Pascal program which defines a subrange of 1 .. 99 for an integer variable FRED. Find out what happens when you assign the value 100 to FRED.

4.7.3   Repeat Exercise 4.7.2 using COBOL.

4.7.4   Use the appropriate manual to discover the value of the largest real number supported by your version of Pascal.

4.7.5   Write a Pascal program to add 1 to the value of MAXINT, to discover what happens.

4.7.6   Write a Pascal program which causes arithmetic underflow in real arithmetic.

4.7.7   Repeat Exercise 4.7.6 using COBOL.

4.7.8   Write a Pascal program which computes 0.3+0.3+0.3 and prints the results. Compare the result with 0.9.

4.7.9   Repeat Exercise 4.7.8 using COBOL.

4.7.10 Use the appropriate manual to find out which character set your computer uses. Then write a Pascal program to print all the possible characters together with the decimal equivalents of their binary patterns.

4.7.11 Write a Pascal program to read in a piece of text, count the number of occurrences of the letters A to Z, and output the counts in the form of a table.

4.7.12 Write a Pascal program to read in a piece of text and output it in reverse order.

4.7.13 Write a Pascal program to read in a piece of text and indicate whether or not it was a palindrome.

4.7.14 Convert the program design of Example 4.2 into Pascal and COBOL.

4.7.15 Convert the program design of Example 4.3 into Pascal and COBOL.

4.7.16 Convert the program design of Example 4.4 into Pascal and COBOL.

4.7.17 Convert the program design of Example 4.5 into Pascal and COBOL.

CHAPTER 5

Debugging and testing

5.1 Introduction □ 5.2 Testing the program design □ 5.3 Syntax and syntax errors □ 5.4 Debugging □ 5.5 Testing □ 5.6 Hints on debugging and testing □ 5.7 Summary □ 5.8 Exercises

5.1 Introduction

This chapter examines the ways in which programs are tested. Approximately one half of the time taken to develop a program is spent in testing, and yet of all the effort devoted to finding ways of improving program production, much less than one half is spent on the testing phase. Perhaps it is not surprising that programmers do not enjoy trying to demonstrate that their programs do not work. More significantly, it is predictable that a programmer in isolation cannot be expected to test his program thoroughly and dispassionately. To improve the quality of testing, it is necessary for standard methods and techniques to be used to devise a testing strategy and to select test data. The purpose of this chapter is to introduce some of these methods and techniques, identifying their role and importance in the overall approach to program testing.

5.2 Testing the program design

Contrary to popular belief among many programmers, testing does not start once the program code has been produced. Testing is just as important during program design as it is during program implementation. Program design cannot be described as finished until the design has been subjected to carefully planned and stringent testing. There is no point in coding a program design that contains errors; the resultant program would certainly not produce the required results. The earlier in the program development cycle that an error is introduced, and the longer it remains undetected, the greater will be the cost of removing the error.

Throughout the development of a program, the programmer must always be aware of the original specification of the required results. The sole objective of testing is to improve the reliability of the program in producing those results. It must be remembered that errors can be introduced by various people: the user who originally stated his requirements, the systems analyst who produced the specification, and the programmer who designed the program. All three people should be involved in testing the program design.

Testing is not simply a matter of

● The programmer ensuring that the program processes his test data according to the specification, and
● The systems analyst satisfying himself that the program behaves according to the requirements stated by the user.

The user may have stated his requirements incorrectly, or incompletely or ambiguously. The analyst may have misinterpreted the user's requirements, or made false assumptions, or simply made a mistake when formalising the specification. Before commencing coding, the programmer must enlist the help of the user and the analyst in testing his program design.

5.2.1 The importance of documentation

The chain of communication from user to systems analyst to programmer, is as prone to error as any other chain of communication involving human beings. The user is normally expert in his application area but ignorant of the jargon and techniques of computer programming. A similar, but opposite, description normally applies to the programmer. One of the functions of the systems analyst is to provide a means of communication between user and programmer. The most effective way the analyst can guard against the information being corrupted during communication is by providing comprehensive written documentation.

Minutes should be kept of all meetings between the analyst and user, and analyst and programmer, but these will probably take the form of informal notes. The analyst should produce at least two formal documents: the first being the statement of requirements by the user, and the second being the specification of the solution by the analyst. Each of these documents must be discussed in detail by the people concerned, and formally agreed as being correct.

Top-down design by successive refinement will help the user to understand at least the top levels in the program design. The first few refinements in the design of a large program are likely to be written free of jargon. At this stage of design, the user can often make a useful contribution to discussions. Indeed, it can be argued that the programmer should not proceed to detailed design until the first few refinements have been discussed by the user and the analyst.

5.2.2 Dry running or desk checking

Dry running, or *desk checking*, is one technique which can be used to test the validity of a program design. It is also applicable to the testing of the other stages of program development. It involves the programmer acting as a computer, laboriously executing his program by hand with a set of test data to determine the results produced. Meticulous notes must be made of the effect of executing each part of the program.

Dry running can be a very tedious business. The programmer must guard against all temptations to short-circuit the procedure. It is all too easy to assume the correctness of a particular part of a program and skip over it. This is particularly true when checking iterations; the temptation is to assume that it will always function correctly. In practice, the termination conditions for a loop are frequently the cause of error. Nevertheless, the programmer should minimise the tedium by choosing sensible test data: the simplest data that will adequately test the program design.

Apart from its laborious nature, the disadvantage of dry running is that, however hard the programmer tries, he cannot remain impartial. He knows what the program is supposed to do and is tempted into believing that that is what it does do. Even if he could remain impartial, the author of the design is unlikely to discover errors in it. A more effective way of testing a design is to involve other people in the checking.

5.2.3 Walkthrough

A *walkthrough* involves the programmer in presenting his program design to a group of people. The level of refinement presented in this way will determine the people in the group. For instance, if only the top few levels are being considered, then the group might sensibly consist of the user and the systems analyst, as described above. If, however, the detailed program design is being presented, then the group should consist of other experienced programmers.

The form of the presentation can also vary considerably. It might be that the programmer formally presents his design together with the rationale behind it. The other members of the group could then ask questions and suggest possible problems. Alternatively, the walkthrough might take the form of a dry run, with everybody participating. In either case, notes should be made of the problems identified so that the programmer can solve them later.

A walkthrough is a very useful technique, but to be successful it needs the cooperation of all participants. The programmer must not be too defensive about his work, and neither should the other group members be unjustly critical. Roles will be reversed when another programmer's work is being tested! When all concerned show a constructive attitude, there are many advantages to this approach; errors are identified early, programmers become aware of each other's work, and can benefit from each other's experience.

5.3 Syntax and syntax errors

During conversion of a program design into high-level language coding, the programmer will inevitably make mistakes. During the translation from source code into machine code, the compiler will detect many of these errors as source code which cannot be translated. The most common errors found in this way include

- Bad spelling and bad punctuation, such as the word 'procedure' misspelt, or a full-stop missing
- The use of variables or paragraph names which have not been defined
- The use of words which are reserved for special purposes in the language

These are examples of *syntax errors*.

When defining a language, be it a programming language like Pascal or a spoken language like English, it is necessary to specify the *syntax* or grammar of the language; that is, the rules to which statements in the language must adhere. The syntax of a language like English is very complex and flexible, and frequently leads to ambiguities which are resolved through the context. Inevitably, the syntax of a programming language is simpler, partly to prevent ambiguity and partly to make the compilation process possible.

An example of a syntax rule is 'The word IF must always be followed by a Boolean expression'. This particular syntax rule is very simple and can be stated clearly and unambiguously in English. In general, however, it is not sensible to use a language as rich and complex as English to define the syntax of another language. There is too much scope for ambiguity and imprecision.

5.3.1 Pascal syntax definition

The syntax of Pascal is defined by means of syntax diagrams. As an example, consider the definition of an identifier shown in Figure 5.1.

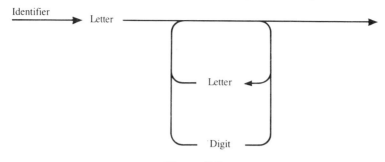

Figure 5.1

To use the diagram, begin at the left and obey the direction of the arrows; at a branching point, go either way. When a word is encountered in the diagram, select an example of what the word represents. The words in a syntax diagram are themselves likely to be the subject of another syntax diagram. To complete the example of Figure 5.1, two further syntax diagrams are needed: one to define 'digit' and one to define 'letter'. The syntax diagram for 'digit' is shown in Figure 5.2.

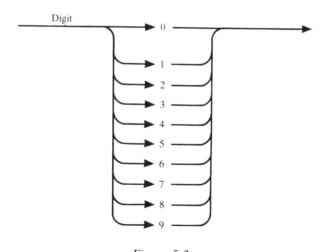

Figure 5.2

The word 'identifier' can then be used in other syntax definitions. For instance, the definition of 'variable declaration' is shown in Figure 5.3.

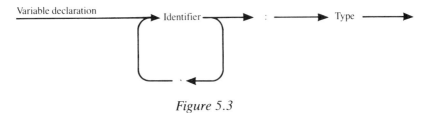

Figure 5.3

The meaning of 'Type' is defined in another syntax diagram. In this way, the syntax rules for the entire language are built up.

5.3.2 COBOL syntax definition

The definitive version of COBOL is ANS (American National Standards) COBOL, and the notation used by ANS for syntax definition has been adopted by most COBOL manuals and textbooks. As an example, consider the definition of an ADD statement in Figure 5.4.

$$\underline{ADD} \quad \begin{Bmatrix} \text{Literal} -1 \\ \text{Identifier} -1 \end{Bmatrix} \quad \begin{bmatrix} \text{Literal} -2 \\ \text{Identifier} -2 \end{bmatrix} \quad \dots \quad \underline{TO}\ \text{identifier-3} \quad \begin{bmatrix} \underline{\text{ROUNDED}} \end{bmatrix}$$

Figure 5.4

The underlined words in capitals are keywords which must be present if a particular language feature is required. Any words in capitals not underlined are optional and are available to improve the readability of the statement. Any words in lower case refer to other definitions. A vertical list of items within a brace indicates that precisely one of those items should appear at that position. A vertical list of items within brackets indicates that precisely one or more of the items may appear at that position. The ellipsis ('. . .') indicates that the immediately preceding item may be repeated any number of times.

Using the above definition of ADD, the following are valid ADD statements:

```
ADD PURCHASES EXPENSES MAINTENANCE
      TO TOTAL-COSTS
ADD X TO Y ROUNDED
ADD 1 TO COUNTER
```

The following are not valid ADD statements:

        ADD A ROUNDED TO B
        ADD PURCHASES EXPENSES MAINTENANCE

5.3.3 Syntax errors

The process of compilation normally produces three things:

● A listing of the original source program
● The corresponding machine code where translation was possible
● Diagnostic messages where syntax errors were found

Sometimes the source listing and the diagnostic messages are intermingled, and sometimes they are separate.

   Diagnostic messages should be clear and unambiguous. They should identify the error found and the position of the error. Position will normally be given in terms of a source program line number and perhaps a character number within statement. For instance, a COBOL compiler might produce the following diagnostic message:

        ★★★LINE 127 CHAR 42 SEVERITY 2 – NON-NUMERIC
                                OPERAND IN ADD
                                STATEMENT

The severity code indicates how serious the error is. Different severity codes may be used to inform the programmer of the action taken by the compiler to overcome the error.

   Not all compilers produce diagnostic messages as good as the above example. Messages of the type

                ERROR 67

are all too common, and cause programmers to reach for the compiler manual to look up the error number. If you have to use a compiler which produces such messages, then complain! A great deal of time and money can be wasted because of such unfriendly software.

   Once the error is identified and located, the programmer must correct the syntax of his program. Once pointed out, most syntax errors are obvious and easily corrected. The less experienced the programmer, the more likely he will have to consult the syntax definition for the language. But syntax definitions do not always tell the full story.

   The diagnostic message 'NON-NUMERIC OPERAND IN ADD STATEMENT' illustrates the difficulty of defining syntax in a formal notation. The statement

ADD 1 TO FRED

satisfies the syntax definition of Figure 5.4 but is meaningless unless FRED is a numeric item. Attached to the formal notation of Figure 5.4, we need a statement to the effect that all literals and identifiers used must represent numeric quantities.

Tracking down a syntax error is sometimes confused by the 'knock-on' effect, where a single error can give rise to many misleading and unnecessary diagnostic messages. For instance, the following erroneous declaration

VAR
BILL : INTERGER;

will give rise to a diagnostic message identifying an illegal type. However, all subsequent uses of BILL are likely to generate a diagnostic message about an undeclared identifier. Sometimes it is not easy to spot where the real error lies.

A program, or compilation, which produces diagnostic messages is described as 'dirty'. Sometimes it may require several recompilations to remove all the syntax errors from a program. When all the syntax errors have been removed, the program, and compilation, is said to be 'clean'.

5.4 Debugging

Once a clean compilation has been obtained, the program enters the *debugging phase*. A *bug* in a program is an error which causes the program either to produce the wrong results or to fail to terminate at all. *Debugging* is the repetitive execution of the program with test data in order to identify, and then correct, the remaining bugs.

Program bugs are often referred to as *logical* or *semantic errors*. The program may be syntactically correct but it produces the wrong results. If a program does not do what the programmer wants it to do, then it is because the programmer has told it to do the wrong thing. One of the biggest problems for the programmer is to remain objective and avoid making any assumptions about his program.

Some bugs will have started off as errors in the program design and been carried through to the implemented program; by this stage most of these errors will have been eliminated. Other bugs will have been introduced by not faithfully translating the program design into coding. Yet more bugs will have appeared as the result of misconceptions about the action of certain statements in the language. The only way to discover these bugs is to check the actual results obtained against the expected results for a set of test data.

5.4.1 Compiler options for semantic error detection

We have already seen how the programmer can help in the detection of run-time logical errors. For example, constraining the possible values of a variable by means of the Pascal subrange facility will enable the compiler to generate machine code to detect at run-time if a variable strays out of range. The error can then be reported immediately to the user of the program. This extra machine code obviously makes the object program larger and reduces the run-time speed.

The generation by the compiler of additional machine code for the purpose of debugging is often made optional to the user. During debugging, it is obviously sensible to have such additional machine code included. Once the program has passed beyond the debugging stage, however, it can be argued that this additional machine code constitutes an unacceptable overhead and should be removed. When initiating a compilation, therefore, it is normal for the programmer to choose which debugging code should be generated by selecting appropriate compiler options.

One diagnostic check which is commonly invoked via a compiler option is an array bounds check for subscripted variables. Suppose a COBOL program contains the following definition:

02 COST OCCURS 10 TIMES.

The only valid references are COST(1), COST(2), . . . , COST(10). When faced with a reference like COST(X), the compiler generates code to calculate the address of the required element, on the assumption that X is in the range 1 to 10. If, at run time, X is outside this range, one of two things may happen.

- The address calculated may be outside the computer's memory or outside that part of memory allocated to the program. In this case, the hardware is likely to detect an *address error* and stop the program.
- The address calculated may be outside the array but within the memory allocated to the program. The effect in this case will depend on which part of the program is accidentally accessed (another variable, an area occupied by a constant or an instruction) and on the operation being performed (reading or writing). It is quite possible that the hardware will detect no error condition.

When addressing arrays of two or more dimensions, it is possible for an individual subscript to be outside its permitted range but the address calculated still to be within the array. In this case, processing will continue but is likely to produce the wrong results.

Optional machine code to check that each subscript is in range would be positioned before the address calculation and would remove the uncertainty about the error being detected. This makes the task of debugging considerably easier.

Diagnostic checks for arithmetic errors are also made subject to a compiler option. For instance, if arithmetic underflow occurs in real arithmetic, the hardware is capable of 'recovering' by setting the value to true zero. The program could then continue execution. For many programs this might be a perfectly acceptable course of action; for other programs, it might lead to consequential knock-on errors. A compiler option could enable the programmer to choose the appropriate reaction to the error.

Even when it is known that a particular type of error will be trapped by the hardware, it may still be sensible to invoke a compiler option to detect it by software. The reason lies in the quality of the error message. If an array subscript out of bounds is detected by the hardware, the error message produced is likely to be general and rather terse, such as

ADDRESS ERROR AT 1E42A

where 1E42A is the hexadecimal address of the machine code instruction being executed at the time of the error. If the same error is detected by software within the program itself, the error message can be much more specific and useful:

ARRAY BOUNDS VIOLATION, LINE 42

The error could be reported in terms of the source program (LINE 42) instead of the machine code program (1E42A). It would be possible for the diagnostic software to identify the array COST and even the subscript X, but this level of error reporting implies considerable storage overheads.

The moral of this section is – find out which debugging options your compiler provides, and use them wherever appropriate.

5.4.2 Error location

When faced with a non-trivial program producing incorrect results, it is not an easy matter to locate the errors. The task of debugging can be simplified by 'defensive' programming during the design and coding phases. If the design is performed by successive refinements, and if the program is systematically constructed from combinations of the three basic constructs sequence, selection and iteration, then the program will naturally divide into components. Each component will perform a specific function within the program and communicate with other components via common variables and data structures. It is therefore possible to test each component fairly independently of the others, by feeding it with correct data and examining its output. The program's internal structure has the effect of confining errors to small areas, thus making them easier to locate.

The simplest way to discover whether a variable is assigned an incorrect value is to include in the program a number of extra output statements. The value of the variable can then be monitored as the execution of the program proceeds. Suppose, for example, it is suspected that the body of a loop is being executed once too often. Figure 5.5 shows a fragment of a Pascal program which uses an additional WRITELN statement to output the number of iterations performed.

```
KOUNT := 1;
WHILE KOUNT <= N DO
BEGIN
        WRITELN (KOUNT);      (*DEBUGGING STATEMENT*)
        .
        .
        .
        KOUNT := KOUNT+1
END;
```

Figure 5.5

The WRITELN statement will obviously affect the intended output format for the program. The programmer must remember to remove it, once debugging is complete, and recompile the program.

The same technique can be used in COBOL with the DISPLAY verb, but COBOL's debugging feature allows statements to remain in the source program even when the debugging phase is complete. Consider again our suspect loop. Figure 5.6 shows some COBOL coding to output the number of iterations.

The D (in character position 7) indicates that the line is a *debugging line*. If the programmer switches debugging ON, then all debugging lines are compiled as normal statements. If the programmer switches debugging OFF, all debugging lines are ignored by the compiler. Debugging can be switched ON or OFF by a single statement near the beginning of the program.

The removal of all the machine code associated with COBOL debugging lines involves a one-line edit followed by a recompilation—much more convenient than the Pascal equivalent. Moreover, the debugging lines themselves need never be removed from the source program. They can remain in place and be reactivated should a bug be discovered later.

```
PERFORM LOOP VARYING KOUNT FROM 1 BY 1
           UNTIL KOUNT > N.
              .
              .
              .
              .
              .
              .
   LOOP.
D       DISPLAY KOUNT.
              .
              .
              .
   NEXT-PARA.
```

Figure 5.6

5.4.3 Error correction

Once an error has been identified and located, it must be corrected. It is at this point that an inexperienced programmer may be tempted to rush into the first alteration that comes into his head. This approach rarely works and normally results in introducing more bugs. Instead, it is necessary to consider carefully the implications and ramifications of any contemplated change. A good deal of desk-checking is needed before the change is made and the program retested.

The error discovered may be a coding error, that is, a mistake made during the conversion of the design into a source program. These errors are usually caused by an incomplete understanding of the programming language, and can be solved by consulting manuals or more experienced programmers. Alternatively, the error may be a logic error in the detailed program design. In this case, it is important not to try to correct the coding, but instead to try to correct the program design. It is important to work down through the successive refinements until the introduction of the erroneous logic is located. The detailed design must then be corrected and finally the source coding adjusted. Program documentation should also be updated.

5.4.4 Debugging aids

We have already seen that the compiler can help in program debugging by providing certain run-time error checks. Other *debugging aids* are available to the user, some provided by the systems software and some manual procedures. The sensible programmer makes use of all the help he can get.

Dry running and desk checking

Equally useful for testing the source coding as they are for testing the program design. A program can be executed by hand using test data and the changes to variables noted on a piece of paper. Dry running a program is a tedious business and prone to all the problems mentioned in Section 5.2.2.

Walkthrough

Such techniques can also be applied to program code. In fact, when a student takes an incorrect program to a lecturer, the lecturer normally conducts a walkthrough of the coding. The student is asked to explain the action of his program to the lecturer, who plays a fairly passive part and merely prompts with questions like 'Why' and 'What if . . .'. Invariably, the student himself finds the bug.

Storage maps and cross-reference listings

These can be produced by the compiler if the programmer requests them. A storage map is simply a list of the variables used in a program. A cross-reference listing is a storage map plus all the line numbers where each variable is used. These two optional listings help the programmer to avoid clashes of use for the variables in his program.

Program traces

Used to show the path of execution through a program. They are normally produced by extra machine code generated via a compiler option. They are invaluable in identifying the range of an infinite loop.

Frequency analysers

Used to show the frequency with which execution passes through the various parts of a program. They can highlight the frequently-used parts and the seldom-used parts, or even whether a particular part has been used at all. If the frequency analysis differs significantly from the pattern of use expected by the programmer, it may indicate loops out of control.

Interactive testing systems

These allow a program to be executed under interactive control by the programmer. The program can be made to stop when it reaches certain statements; variables can then be inspected, and even changed, by the programmer before the program is allowed to continue. Many other facilities are available in a modern interactive testing system, and can considerably reduce the time spent in debugging.

5.5 Testing

Testing is the process of repeatedly executing a program with different sets of data. The objective of testing is to demonstrate that the program satisfies its specification, that is, that the program is correct. However, for all non-trivial programs, no amount of testing can show that a program is correct. A test-run can only prove the presence of bugs, it cannot prove their absence. Each test-run which fails to detect a bug can only serve to increase our confidence in a program.

Since testing can never demonstrate absolute correctness, we must adopt a sensible and systematic approach to testing in order to maximise our confidence in the program. If a program can be logically split into separate components, it is advisable to concentrate the testing on one component at a time. This may affect the way in which the program is developed.

Consider, for example, a program which has a data-vetting section followed by a data-processing section. It may be possible to test two versions of the program in parallel: one version with a complete data-vetting section and a dummy data-processing section, the other version with a complete data-processing section and a dummy data-vet. The two halves could be joined together later for some final program testing. Testing the entire program as one entity from the start would have been more difficult since there are so many potential sources of error.

5.5.1 Choice of test data

Choosing test data at random is almost a complete waste of time. In general, programmers give insufficient thought and time to the devising of a testing strategy and the choice of test data. Testing is an integral part of program development, and proper testing is as intellectually challenging as any other part.

Test data should be chosen systematically. Each set of test data should have a particular objective. These objectives are best identified during the program design stage, though the generation of the test data itself may be left until later. Before the test is carried out, the expected results should be produced by hand. Without knowing the expected results in advance, it is all too easy to believe that the actual results are correct. It should be noted, however, that hand calculation of the expected results is not always easy. Where the problem being solved is extremely complex and lengthy, it may not be practical or even possible for a human being to calculate the expected results.

The generation of actual values for test data can be a time-consuming and boring job. This is partly the reason for program testing being done badly. *Test data generators* are designed to take the tedium out of this process. They are pieces of software which, in simple terms, accept a description of the data required and then produce multiple examples of it. Consider, for example, the following description of an item of data:

type	:	integer
number of digits	:	3
valid values	:	100, 150 through 450

To test that a program handles this item of data correctly we need to use values like 149, 150, 450 and 451 to test the boundary conditions, and 100 to test the isolated value. We also need to test for 2-digit numbers, 1-digit numbers, non-integer numbers, and non-numeric values. A test data generator could create such values for us, in combination with values for other items of data. Of course, the generator would need to know the relative positions of each item of data in the data file.

The one thing that a test data generator cannot do is to tell us what the expected results are for each set of data. The actual results produced need to be checked very carefully. The value of test data generators is therefore limited.

5.5.2 Black box testing

There are two fundamentally different approaches to testing a program. *Black box testing* ignores the internal construction of a program and concentrates on the input values and output results.

The programmer should analyse each item of data and decide what constitutes a valid value and an invalid value. There may be several ways in which a value may be invalid: it may be of the wrong type, too large, too small, too long, too short, or simply missing. Similarly, it may be possible to identify several different values, or ranges of values, for which the data item is valid. It is necessary to choose test data which will test all eventualities. Particular attention should be paid to the boundaries between valid and invalid values.

A similar approach can be applied to output values. Input values should be chosen to generate the full range of output values. For instance maximum and minimum values should be induced in numeric output variables in order to test the output editing. Similarly, maximum and minimum length strings should be induced in character variables in order to test output layouts.

Finally, it must be remembered that a program should not fail, irrespective of how much the actual data varies from the expected data. A common failure is caused by too much or too little data. For example, many programs fail when presented with an empty data file.

5.5.3 White box testing

The objective of *white box testing* is to construct test data which will ensure that every path through the program is tested. This obviously involves a close examination of the source code, concentrating on the points where conditions are located, such as IF statements and loop control. A condition indicates that the path of execution will branch into one of two alternative directions. With white box testing, we have to ensure that at some stage during testing, both paths are followed. This means that the data has to be chosen to ensure that every condition is 'true' at least once and 'false' at least once.

Complete black box testing would require every combination of invalid data to be included in the test. The advantage of white box testing is that the internal arrangement of the coding tells us which combinations are worth testing and which are not. The large number of combinations possible sometimes makes complete black box testing impractical. Most programmers use a combination of black box and white box testing.

5.6 Hints on debugging and testing

To a novice programmer, the task of debugging and thoroughly testing a complex program can be daunting. As he gains experience, the programmer will build up memories of the mistakes he has made and corrected in the past. Nowadays, no programming error is intrinsically new; it will have appeared already, perhaps in a modified form, in some earlier program. Expertise in debugging and testing is developed through experience and by talking to other programmers. There is no real substitute for experience.

It is impossible to give an exhaustive list of the variations in errors that can occur in a program. However, some errors do occur more frequently than others, especially in programs written by inexperienced programmers, and the following list of hints is intended to guide a programmer towards some of the more common ones.

(1)   Use DISPLAY statements (COBOL) and WRITE/WRITELN statements (Pascal) in order to
   ● Output the values of variables as execution proceeds
   ● Trace the path of execution through a program by identifying certain statements as they are reached
(2)   Output the value of all data immediately after they are input. This is

called *echo-printing*.
(3) Validate all data; never assume it is within range.
(4) Make sure your program does something sensible when presented with an empty data file. Failing with a run-time error, or stopping without producing any output, is not sensible.
(5) Check the definition of your numeric variables, particularly in COBOL, to avoid
   ● Arithmetic overflow
   ● Unwanted truncation
   ● Loss of significance
(6) In Pascal, use subranges wherever appropriate.
(7) Avoid the direct comparison of REAL values. Instead, compare their difference with a small constant which represents the tolerance.
(8) Use parentheses to make arithmetic expressions and Boolean expressions clear and unambiguous.
(9) Use indentations to clarify the range of
   ● The body of a loop (Pascal in particular)
   ● The statements subordinate to an IF statement
(10) Use comments liberally throughout your code to remind you what your code is intended to do.
(11) In Pascal, remember that if the CASE selector does not match one of the alternatives then the action of the CASE statement is undefined.
(12) In Pascal, remember that after exit from a FOR loop, the value of the loop control variable is undefined.
(13) Check that you have not inadvertently created a recursive calling sequence. Such a sequence is invalid in COBOL. It is valid in Pascal, but may not be what you intended.
(14) When using procedures in Pascal or external subprograms in COBOL, ensure that the formal parameter list matches the actual parameter list with respect to
   ● The number of parameters
   ● The order of parameters
   ● The type of parameters
(15) From within a Pascal procedure, only make reference to its own formal parameters and local variables. Never refer to global variables.

5.7 Summary

Testing is an extremely important phase in the program development cycle. Computers are being used in an ever increasing variety of applications, many of which are outside the traditional data-processing environment. The need for correct and reliable operation is more important than ever before; testing is one of the few ways of directly measuring correctness and reliability. Once the testing is considered complete, and the program is handed over, the next quality control checks are performed by the user. If he is not satisfied with what he gets, he has every right to complain.

5.8 Exercises

5.8.1   Obtain copies of the Pascal and COBOL syntax definitions. They will prove invaluable during program testing.

5.8.2   Discover which options your Pascal and COBOL compilers offer you for run-time error detection, and find out how to use them.

5.8.3   Identify suitable test data and expected results for the programs you wrote for Exercise 4.7.14.

5.8.4   Identify suitable test data and expected results for the programs you wrote for Exercise 4.7.15.

5.8.5   Identify suitable test data and expected results for the programs you wrote for Exercise 4.7.16.

5.8.6   Identify suitable test data and expected results for the programs you wrote for Exercise 4.7.17.

5.8.7   Identify suitable test data and expected results for a program which calculates INCOMETAX from GROSSPAY. Tax is deducted according to the following rules:
(1) The first £5000 is tax free
(2) The next £3000 is taxed at 35%
(3) The next £5000 is taxed at 45%
(4) The remainder is taxed at 65%

CHAPTER 6

A method of structured design

6.1 Introduction □ 6.2 What is a structured program? □ 6.3 Data structures □ 6.4 From data structures to program structures □ 6.5 Schematic logic □ 6.6 Summary

6.1 Introduction

The approach to program design adopted so far in this book has been stepwise refinement; involving the splitting of a problem into its constituent parts. This decomposition is performed repetitively until the resulting components are sufficiently small and simple to code. As an aid in the process of decomposition, a simple structure diagram notation has been used, based on three fundamental programming constructs: sequence, selection and iteration.

This approach is perfectly adequate for the relatively simple problems considered so far. However, as increasingly complex problems are considered, it becomes obvious that the success of simple stepwise refinement depends on the ability to 'see' an outline solution in the first place. What has been done so far is to formalise the decomposition of the problem so that mistakes are less likely to be made during the refinement of an outline solution.

What must be considered is how to proceed when there is no 'obvious' solution. What is needed is a systematic method of program design which can be applied to any problem and which will help produce a program design to solve that problem. Such a method is Jackson Structured Programming, developed in America in the early 1970s and described by M. A. Jackson in his book *Principles of Program Design*. This chapter introduces the Jackson Structured Programming (JSP) method.

6.2 What is a structured program?

A program normally has a single function. For instance, a program which produces weekly pay-slips from an employee masterfile will do just that and nothing more. If it is necessary for the masterfile records to be in a particular order before the pay-slips can be produced, the sorting will be achieved by using a separate program. The programs are separate in the sense that they are compiled independently of each other, but they collaborate with each other as a *system* of programs to achieve an overall objective. Each program within a system of collaborating programs is normally called a *module*, and the practice of using a system of programs to solve a problem is called *modular programming*.

Modular programming should not be confused with structured programming. Structured programming is concerned with the internal design of a program and not with its relationship to other external programs. We will use the word *component* to mean any element of a program structure: program, subprogram, section, procedure, paragraph, function, even program statement. The word module will only be used to indicate a separately compiled program.

At this point it is well worth emphasising that it is the programmers who benefit from structured programming, not the computer. At run-time it makes no difference to the computer hardware whether the program is structured or not. Indeed, the use of structured programming techniques to develop a program is likely to cause the machine-code program to be larger and run more slowly than is strictly necessary. This slight inefficiency at run-time is more than compensated for by the improved reliability, readability and maintainability of the source program.

Any component of a well structured program will have the following properties.

- *As few subcomponents as possible*
  Each component must be fully and clearly understood. This is not possible if a component consists of many subcomponents. Psychological surveys have found that the human mind is capable of handling only 7 ± 2 objects or concepts simultaneously. This gives us guidance as to the number of subcomponents into which we should split each component at successive refinements of the program design. At the final stage of refinement, the subcomponents created will correspond to statements in the implementation language.
- *A simple control structure*
  We have already introduced and used the permissible control structures: sequence, selection and iteration. Using just these three control structures, it is possible to define the solution to any problem, that is, they are sufficient on their own and we do not need to consider others.

The main advantage of these three control structures is that they are easy to understand.

● *One entry and one exit*

If a component has a simple control structure, and it is possible to split the component into several subcomponents, and each subcomponent has a simple control structure, then it follows that each subcomponent (and therefore each component) must have only one entry and exit. This property improves the readability of a component and makes it easier to understand.

● *No side-effects*

A component must perform the operations specified for it, but it is equally important that the component does no more than that. Variables not mentioned in the specification should not be altered by the execution of the component. This may seem obvious but it is crucially important: we cannot understand the action of a component if we cannot rely on its subcomponents having this property.

6.3 Data structures

Jackson Structured Programming is based on analysing the structure of the given input data and the structure of the required output data. This information is then used as the basis for the design of the program structure. JSP, therefore, requires a clear and simple notation which can be used to display the structure of data and programs alike. The structures used to define programs (that is, sequence, selection and iteration) turn out to be equally suitable for the description of data. In fact, it could be argued that the concepts have been introduced in the wrong order. The purpose of a program is to process data. If sequence, selection and iteration were not suitable constructs for describing data then they could not be suitable for defining programs.

The structure diagrams used so far to describe programs could be used equally well to describe data. However, at this point a widely-used notation which has become an industry standard can be introduced: the *JSP structure diagram*.

6.3.1 Sequence

Figure 6.1 shows an example of sequence.

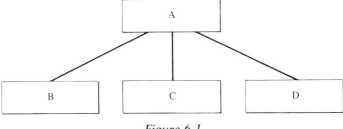

Figure 6.1

This means that A consists of a B, followed by a C, followed by a D. The order is significant. Examples of sequence in data structures are given in Figure 6.2.

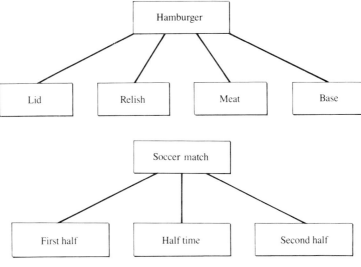

Figure 6.2

6.3.2 Selection

Figure 6.3 shows an example of selection.

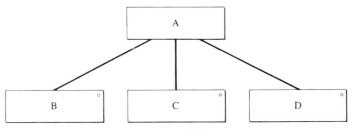

Figure 6.3

This means that A consists of one of B or C or D. There must be two or more possibilities. Examples of selection in data structures are given in Figure 6.4.

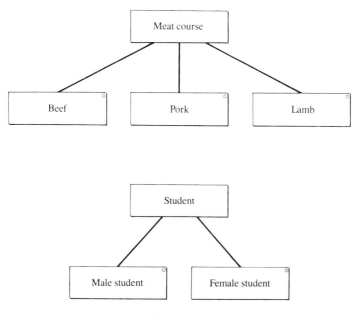

Figure 6.4

It does not matter if there are other possibilities for a 'meat course'. It must be assumed that in a particular situation the only possibilities are the three shown.

6.3.3 Iteration

Figure 6.5 shows an example of iteration.

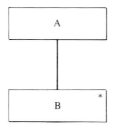

Figure 6.5

This means that A consists of zero or more Bs. Examples of iteration in data structures are given in Figure 6.6.

Figure 6.6

Note that the name in the iterated box should always be singular. For instance, 'group' consists of zero or more repetitions of 'student', not 'students'. Failure to observe this rule will often result in confusion about what is meant.

6.3.4 The constructs in combination

Structure diagrams using the notation introduced in Chapter 2 tend to grow from left to right across the page as more detail is added. JSP structure diagrams, on the other hand, tend to grow from top to bottom down the page. Each new refinement of the diagram tends to add one or more boxes in a new line at the bottom of the diagram.

Example 6.1

Let us consider the definition of a bookshelf. The first refinement is trivial, as shown in Figure 6.7.

Figure 6.7

The next refinement, shown in Figure 6.8, defines the bookshelf as a line of books with a book-end at each end.

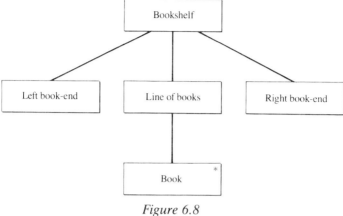

Figure 6.8

A further refinement might be to define a book as either a hardback or a paperback, as shown in Figure 6.9.

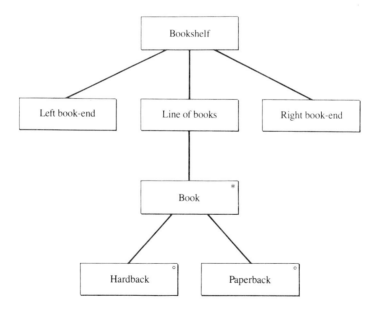

Figure 6.9

Obviously, this is not the only way to define a bookshelf. For instance, it may be more important to classify a book as 'fact' or 'fiction'. The definition to be used should be evident from the context of the problem.

Example 6.2

Figure 6.10 shows the definition of a data file describing a group of students. Each record in the file relates to a particular student, and the last student record is followed by a special trailer record.

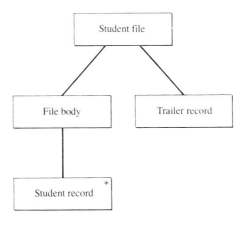

Figure 6.10

Each student record will contain several different pieces of information: name, address, sex, age, etc. All of these items of data could be shown as a sequence beneath 'Student Record'. This would be necessary if the implementation language demanded that the internal organisation of a record should be considered. For instance, one item at a time could be read in Pascal, in which case the order of the items in the record is obviously important. In COBOL, on the other hand, a complete record could be read giving direct access to all data items; in such circumstances the internal organisation of the record does not have to be specified in the structure diagram.

The way in which a file is to be processed may, however, make it sensible to classify the records in a particular way. Suppose, for instance, that it is necessary to identify for special treatment those students who are mature, that is, over the age of 20. A suitable structure diagram is given in Figure 6.11.

6.4 From data structures to program structures

Having established how to use JSP structure diagrams to describe the structure of the data being input to a program and the structure of the data being output, a systematic method for using these data structure definitions to produce a structure diagram for the program is now required. This method involves a number of phases.

Phase 1:   Write down the data structures
Phase 2:   Combine the data structures
Phase 3:   Allocate label names
Phase 4:   Add the conditions
Phase 5:   List the actions
Phase 6:   Allocate the actions

The following example illustrates what is involved in each of these phases.

Example 6.3

Start with the data file of student details, as described in Figure 6.11, and design a program to print the names of all mature students. In addition to this, the program is required to produce a count of the number of male mature students and a count of the number of female mature students.

Phase 1: Write down the data structures

The diagram of Figure 6.11 must be extended in order to differentiate between male mature students and female mature students. The structure of the output file must also be defined. Figure 6.12 shows suitable structure diagrams for the data and results of this program.

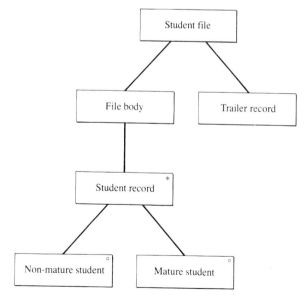

Figure 6.11

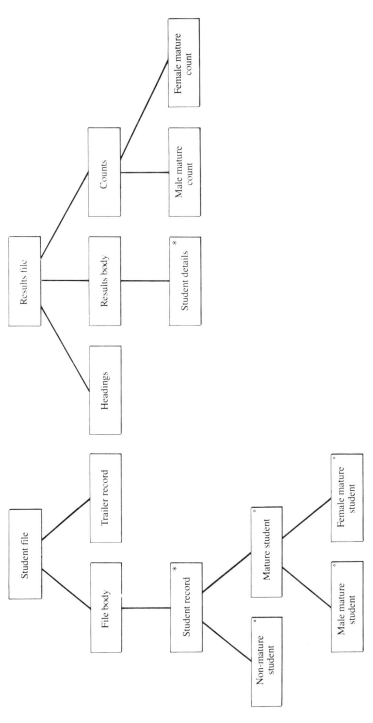

Figure 6.12

Phase 2: Combine the data structures

The data structures must be combined into a single structure which can then be developed into the program structure. In order to combine two, or more, data structures into a single structure, *correspondences* must be identified, that is, we must identify in the diagrams, boxes which correspond to each other. This is best achieved by considering in turn each box in the input data structure, starting at the top and working from left to right within each level. If, when processing the data component represented by a box in the input data structure, the program produces the data component represented by a box in the output data structure, then such a correspondence has been identified.

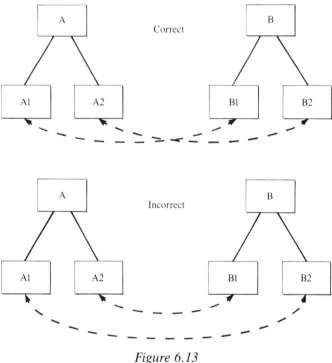

Figure 6.13

The following guidelines will help to identify the boxes which correspond:

● A box in one data structure can correspond to no more than one box in another data structure. It may correspond to none at all.
● Two boxes can correspond only if the data components they represent occur the same number of times. For instance, in Figure 6.12, 'student record' and 'student details' do not correspond since not all students produce an output line.

● Boxes in a sequence in the input data structure can correspond to boxes in a sequence in the output data structure only if the sequences are the same. Figure 6.13 gives examples of correct and incorrect correspondence of sequences. This restriction does not apply where selection, as opposed to sequence, is the relationship between boxes. For instance, Figure 6.14 shows a possible correct situation.

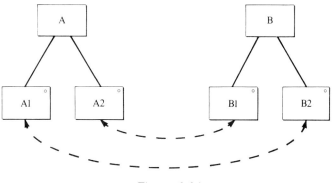

Figure 6.14

Applying these guidelines to the data structures of Figure 6.12, four correspondences can be established. These are shown in Figure 6.15.

The structures can now be combined. When combining structures, there are two golden rules to observe.

● If two boxes correspond, they will share a single box in the combined structure. If a box does not have a corresponding partner, it will have a separate box to itself in the combined structure.
● The structure of the files being combined must be maintained in the combined structure. By erasing some of the boxes in the combined structure, it must be possible to produce the structure of each constituent file.

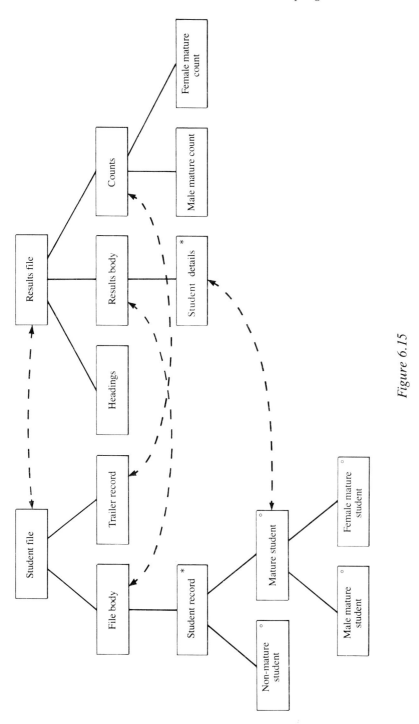

Figure 6.15

By combining the two structures of Figure 6.15, the outline program structure of Figure 6.16 is obtained.

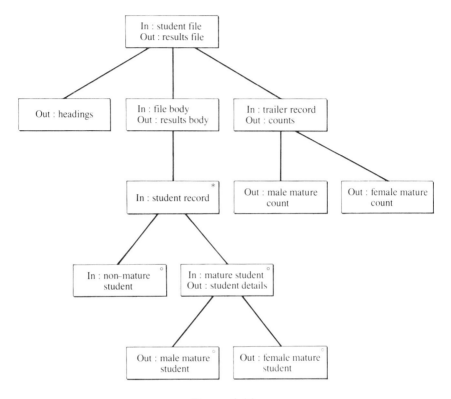

Figure 6.16

Phase 3: Allocate label names

During this phase, each box in the outline program structure is examined and the function it is to perform in the final program identified. A name or phrase is then created to describe that function. These names or phrases must be chosen with extreme care. They must be as concise as possible, while still conveying the precise function of the associated program component. The correct choice of these names or phrases has a significant effect on the readability, and hence on the maintainability, of the program.

Figure 6.17 shows the program structure with suitable label names allocated.

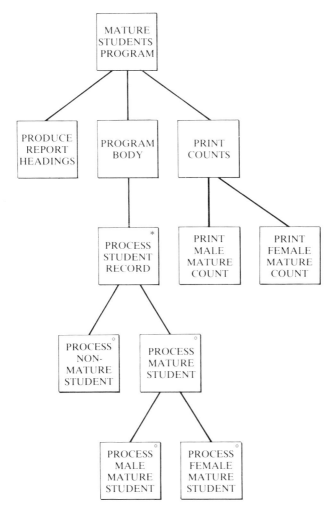

Figure 6.17

Phase 4: Add the conditions

The execution of program components that represent a selection or an iteration is governed by a condition. During this phase these conditions are added to the diagram. At this stage, the temptation to descend into a particular programming language notation should be avoided; these particular conditions should be written in clear and unambiguous English. The conditions are written above the box to which they relate.

Figure 6.18 shows the program structure with suitable conditions attached.

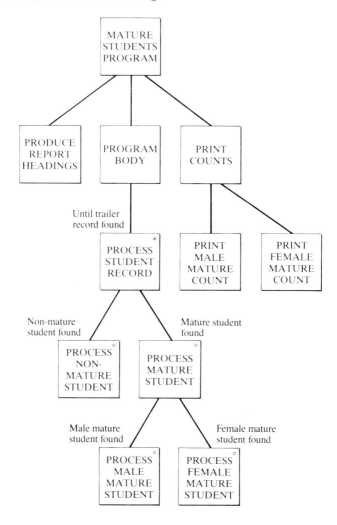

Figure 6.18

Phase 5: List the actions

During this phase, a numbered list is made of all the actions the program needs to perform, making no attempt to place the actions in any particular order. Once again, expressing the actions in a programming language notation should be avoided; the actions should be specified in clear, unambiguous English.

A list of necessary actions for the example program is given in Figure 6.19.

1.	Open input file
2.	Open output file
3.	Stop program
4.	Read an input record
5.	Output headings to results file
6.	Output student details line to results file
7.	Output male mature count to results file
8.	Output female mature count to results file
9.	Increment male mature count
10.	Increment female mature count
11.	Initialise male mature count to zero
12.	Initialise female mature count to zero
13.	Close input file
14.	Close output file

Figure 6.19

Phase 6: Allocate the actions

In this phase, each action must be allocated to one or more components in the program structure. Actions invariably describe operations performed upon a piece of data, and should therefore, if possible, be allocated to the program component which corresponds to the original data component. For example, action 9 relates to the count of male mature students which relates to the data component 'male mature student' which corresponds to program component PROCESS MALE MATURE STUDENT; obviously, action 9 should be allocated to this program component. However, action 11 also relates to the data component 'male mature student' but should not be allocated to the program component PROCESS MALE MATURE STUDENT because action 11 must be executed only once. At first sight, there is no obvious program component to which action 11 should be allocated. The same applies to actions 1, 2, 3 and 12. More will be said about these actions later.

Normally, actions are allocated to elementary components, that is, components which have no subordinate component. This allows non-elementary components to be dedicated to the control functions within a program: sequence, selection and iteration. Sometimes there is a choice of components for the allocation of an action. For example, action 6 could be allocated to either

PROCESS MATURE STUDENT

or both   PROCESS MALE MATURE STUDENT
PROCESS FEMALE MATURE STUDENT

In both cases, the program would function correctly but the second option is the better choice.

When allocating more than one action to a program component, it is necessary to consider very carefully the order in which the action should be specified. Sometimes, the order of two particular actions may be immaterial. For instance, in the example program, the order of actions 1 and 2 is of no consequence; what is important is that they both take place before any other actions involving input/output.

Writing the actions beneath the program component to which they have been allocated produces the program structure of Figure 6.20.

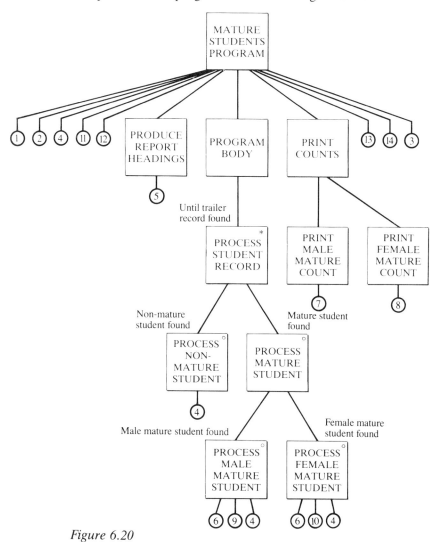

Figure 6.20

Consider again actions 1, 2, 3, 11 and 12. They are all related to the initialisation or termination of the program, and not directly to the processing of the data. Since JSP is based on deriving program structures from data structures, it is perhaps not surprising that the 'housekeeping' actions have no natural home. What must be done is to extend the sequence controlled by the highest level component to include subcomponents for initialisation and termination.

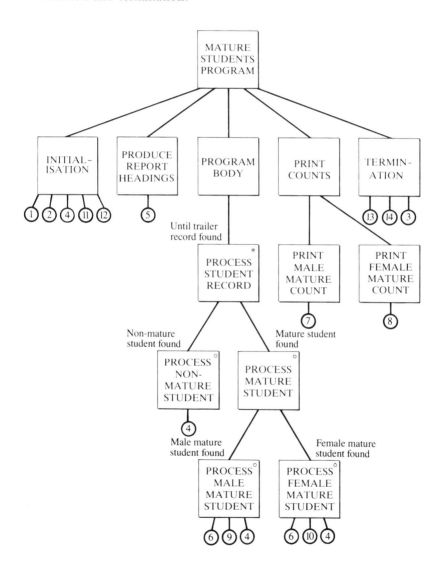

Figure 6.21

Finally, consider the allocation of action 4 (read an input record). The program structure clearly requires an input record to have been read before the first execution of component PROGRAM BODY. Similarly, the next input record must be read before the next execution of PROGRAM BODY. Consequently, use has been made of the read-ahead technique, introduced in Example 3.4, and action 4 has been allocated as shown.

The final program structure is shown in Figure 6.21.

6.5 Schematic logic

It is possible to take the detailed program design of Figure 6.21 and convert it directly into program code. M. A. Jackson himself, however, recommends the use of an intermediate stage to simplify the conversion process. He suggests that the program design first be converted into *schematic logic*, and then the schematic logic converted into the required programming language.

Schematic logic is itself a simple language, the purpose of which is to describe programs. Consequently, the schematic logic constructs correspond to the constructs of a program: seq for sequence, sel for selection and iter for iteration. Each component in the detailed program design is converted into a seq, sel or iter component in the schematic logic. The end of each component is indicated by a corresponding end component. Where components are nested within the schematic logic, indentation is used to help identify the range of each component and its relationship to other components. As a further aid to readability, the beginning and end of each component are given the name of the corresponding component in the program structure diagram.

The general format for a sequence component is shown in Figure 6.22.

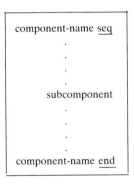

Figure 6.22

The general format of a selection component is shown in Figure 6.23.

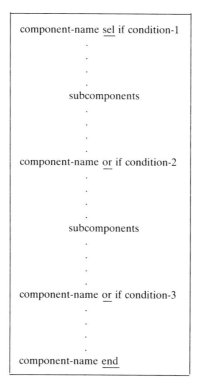

Figure 6.23

The number of <u>or</u> constructs depends on the number of components in the selection.

The general format of an iteration component is shown in Figure 6.24.

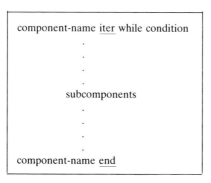

Figure 6.24

The while condition may be replaced by an until condition if it is more convenient.

The schematic logic corresponding to the mature student's program is given in Figure 6.25.

```
MAT-STUD-PROG seq
    Open input file
    Open output file
    Read an input record
    Initialise male mature count to zero
    Initialise female mature count to zero
    Output headings to results file
    PROGRAM-BODY iter until trailer record
        STUDENT-REC sel if non-mature student
            Read an input record
        STUDENT-REC or if mature student
            MAT-STUDENT sel if male mature student
                MALE-MAT-STUD seq
                    Output student details line to results file
                    Increment male mature count
                    Read an input record
                MALE-MAT-STUD end
            MAT-STUDENT or if female mature student
                FEMALE-MAT-STUD seq
                    Output student details line to results file
                    Increment female mature count
                    Read an input record
                FEMALE-MAT-STUD end
            MAT-STUDENT end
        STUDENT-REC end
    PROGRAM-BODY end
    Output male mature count to results file
    Output female mature count to results file
    Close input file
    Close output file
MAT-STUD-PROG end
```

Figure 6.25

6.6 Summary

This chapter has presented the novice programmer with a systematic method of producing the design of a structured program. The design phase is arguably the most critical of all the phases of program development; it is certainly the most difficult phase intellectually. Experienced programmers can often produce a well designed program simply because they have solved similar problems in the past. It is usually a waste of time for an inexperienced programmer to stare at input and output specifications and wait for inspiration. The objective of this chapter has been to remove some of the unpredictability from program design, making it more of a science and less of a mystic art.

CHAPTER 7

Advanced data structures

7.1 Introduction □ 7.2 Physical and logical data structures □ 7.3 Linear lists □ 7.4 Trees □ 7.5 Records □ 7.6 Files □ 7.7 Summary □ 7.8 Exercises

7.1 Introduction

In Chapter 4 the elementary data types were introduced: integers, reals, Booleans and characters. It was then demonstrated how these elementary data types can be grouped together to form simple data structures called vectors and arrays. In this chapter some other ways of structuring data will be examined. Some of the data structures introduced will be groupings of homogeneous data items, as was the case with vectors and arrays. Other data structures introduced here will be collections of different types of data items. As the chapter progresses, structures of increasing complexity will be encountered, and it will be demonstrated how one data structure may be created from components which are themselves previously defined data structures.

7.2 Physical and logical data structures

Physical data structures are those which can be represented directly by the hardware of the computer. Integers, reals, Booleans and characters obviously fall into this category. It can be argued that the one-dimensional array is also a physical data structure. The elements of a vector can be directly mapped onto consecutive locations in a linear memory. Moreover, references of the form

LIST [10]

that is, the 10th item in a vector called LIST, have an almost direct counterpart in most machine codes.

All other data structures are logical, and have to be constructed from combinations of simpler data structures. For example, a two-dimensional array can be thought of as a collection of one-dimensional arrays. Later on in this chapter, it will be demonstrated that a queue can be constructed either from a vector or from a singly-linked list. Once a particular data structure has been defined, it can be used as a building block in the construction of a more complex data structure.

Associated with a data structure, there is a set of operations which can be performed upon it. The operations associated with physical data structures tend to be rather simple in nature, normally storing and retrieving data. As the data structures become more and more distanced from the underlying hardware, so the operations become more and more sophisticated. Some high-level languages explicitly provide these operations for certain data structures, but the programmer often has to code them himself. The algorithms involved will be considered as we examine each data structure.

7.3 Linear lists

A *linear list* is an ordered sequence of data items. There may be zero or more items in the sequence. A linear list is one of the most simple, and yet one of the most useful, of all data structures.

Diagrammatically, a list may be written as

$$I_1, I_2, I_3, \ldots, I_n$$

where each I is an element in the list. Note that each item except one (the first) has a unique predecessor and that each item except one (the last) has a unique successor.

A number of operations are commonly associated with data items stored in a linear list. Some of the common ones are:

- Count the number of items
- Find a particular item in the list
- Replace an item in the list
- Delete an item from the list
- Insert a new item into the list

In any particular application of linear lists, some or all of these operations will be needed. The subset of operations needed for a particular application will help to determine the most appropriate way of implementing the list.

For instance, if the Delete and Insert operations are required, then a vector is not a suitable data structure in which to represent a list. The simpler the operations required, the simpler the mapping to storage can be made.

One of the most obvious ways of implementing a linear list is by means of vector. List item I_j is allocated to the vector element with a subscript value of j, as shown in Figure 7.1.

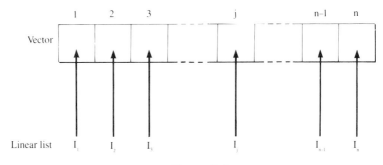

Figure 7.1

This is known as *sequential mapping*, and facilitates equal access to any of the items in the list. Consider again the set of possible actions for a linear list. Only the Delete and Insert operations would cause problems. Deletion would require the emptied element to be closed up; insertion would require an empty element to be created; both operations would result in the moving of some of the other elements in the list in order to maintain the sequential mapping. In many applications, *non-sequential mappings* must be considered in order to avoid this overhead.

Two types of linear list which are commonly used are stacks and queues.

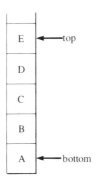

Figure 7.2

7.3.1 Stacks (onto vectors)

A *stack* is a linear list having items that may be added and deleted at only one end, called the *top*. The other end of the stack, the *bottom*, is completely inaccessible. A stack is sometimes referred to as a Last In First Out (LIFO) list. Suppose that the items A, B, C, D, E are inserted into a stack, in that order. Figure 7.2 shows the situation.

If the items are now removed from the stack, they will reappear in reverse order, that is, E, D, C, B, A.

The simplest way to represent a stack is by means of a sequential mapping onto a vector. Consider the following Pascal definitions

```
TYPE
        STACKSIZE = 1 .. MAXSTACKSIZE;
        POINTERTYPE = 0 .. MAXSTACKSIZE;
        STACKTYPE = ARRAY [STACKSIZE] OF ITEMS;
VAR
        TOP    : POINTERTYPE;
        STACK : STACKTYPE;
```

where ITEMS is a type defining the contents of each stack item and MAXSTACKSIZE is a constant defining the maximum number of stack items. The variable TOP 'points' to the current top of the stack. With the stack initially empty, TOP would be initialised to zero. Once the stack has been initialised, two operations are needed in order to use it.

Adding an item

This is often called *pushing* an item onto the stack. The potential problem here is *stack overflow*, that is, attempting to push more than MAXSTACKSIZE items onto the stack. A suitable Pascal procedure is shown in Figure 7.3. Notice how the procedure body does not refer to global variables, that is, variables defined outside the procedure. This makes it impossible for the procedure to have any hidden side effects.

STACKOVERFLOW is a procedure which deals with the stack overflow condition. In practice, it is likely to have parameters, and its function will vary according to the situation in which the stack is being used.

A typical call of this procedure would be

PUSH (DATAITEM, STACK, TOP) ;

where DATAITEM is of type ITEMS.

```
PROCEDURE PUSH (ITEMCOPY : ITEMS;
                VAR STACKCOPY : STACKTYPE;
                VAR TOPCOPY : POINTERTYPE);
BEGIN
      IF TOPCOPY = MAXSTACKSIZE THEN
            STACKOVERFLOW
      ELSE
      BEGIN
            TOPCOPY := TOPCOPY + 1;
            STACKCOPY [TOPCOPY] := ITEMCOPY
      END
END (*PUSH*);
```

Figure 7.3

Removing an item

This involves removing the item at the top of the stack and returning it to
the calling program. This operation is often called *popping* an item from
the stack. The potential problem here is *stack underflow*, that is, attempting
to pop an item from an empty stack. Figure 7.4 shows a suitable Pascal
procedure.

```
PROCEDURE POP   (VAR ITEMCOPY : ITEMS;
                VAR STACKCOPY : STACKTYPE;
                VAR TOPCOPY : POINTERTYPE);
BEGIN
      IF TOPCOPY = 0 THEN
            STACKUNDERFLOW
      ELSE
      BEGIN
            ITEMCOPY := STACKCOPY [TOPCOPY];
            TOPCOPY := TOPCOPY - 1
      END
END (*POP*);
```

Figure 7.4

Whether stack underflow is a valid or invalid condition will depend on the
particular application of the stack. A typical call of the procedure would
be

POP (DATAITEM, STACK, TOP) ;

with DATAITEM receiving the popped item.

We have shown that mapping a stack onto a vector is quite straightforward. The main decision to be taken is how large to make the vector, that is, what value to give MAXSTACKSIZE in the above example. If we make MAXSTACKSIZE too small, stack overflow is likely to occur. If we make it too large, storage is being wasted. The problem is compounded in applications requiring two or more stacks simultaneously.

Take the case of two stacks. Each could be allocated to a separate vector. A more economical approach is to map both onto the same vector, one stack growing from each end. This situation is shown in Figure 7.5.

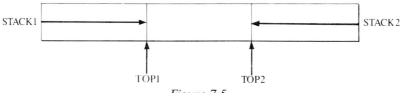

STACK1   STACK2

TOP1   TOP2

Figure 7.5

If the nature of the application is such that the two stacks do not necessarily grow and contract at the same time as each other, this approach can lead to savings in the total storage required. Stack overflow occurs when the pushing of a new item onto one of the stacks would cause the two top pointers to coincide. Assuming appropriate data definitions, Figure 7.6 shows a suitable procedure for pushing an item onto one of the stacks.

```
PROCEDURE PUSHASTACK (ITEMCOPY : ITEMS;
                      VAR STACKCOPY : STACKTYPE;
                      STACKNO : INTEGER;
                      VAR TOP1COPY, TOP2COPY : POINTERTYPE);
BEGIN
        IF TOP1COPY + 1 = TOP2COPY THEN
            STACKOVERFLOW
        ELSE
        BEGIN
            IF STACKNO = 1 THEN
            BEGIN
                (*Add item to first stack *)
                TOP1COPY := TOP1COPY + 1
                STACKCOPY [TOP1COPY] := ITEMCOPY
            END
            ELSE
            BEGIN
                (*Add item to second stack *)
                TOP2COPY := TOP2COPY - 1;
                STACKCOPY [TOP2COPY] := ITEMCOPY
            END
        END
END (*PUSHASTACK*);
```

Figure 7.6

To push an item onto STACK1, a typical call would be

PUSHASTACK (DATAITEM, STACK, 1, TOP1, TOP2);

To push an item onto STACK2, a typical call would be

PUSHASTACK (DATAITEM, STACK, 2, TOP1, TOP2);

The corresponding procedure for popping an item from one of the stacks is left as an exercise. See Exercise 7.8.2.

While being more economical on storage, this approach makes the point at which a particular stack will overflow unpredictable. When considering the case of more that two stacks coexisting in a single vector, the situation becomes even more complicated. The most sensible approach here is to make all stacks grow in the same direction. Figure 7.7 shows the situation for four stacks.

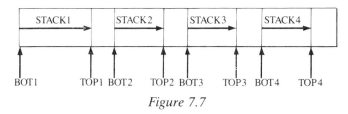

Figure 7.7

The algorithms for pushing and popping are not particularly complex. However, dealing with a stack overflow is difficult since some or all of the stacks must be shifted up or down the vector in order to create some room. This moving around of stacks is a considerable overhead. A simpler solution is to use a linked list as the storage structure for each stack.

7.3.2 Linked lists

The sequential mapping of a linear list onto a vector has been considered already, and it has been noted that the operations of insertion and deletion are not well supported by this mapping. It has also been seen that when we need to store a number of stacks within a single vector, the sequential mapping approach introduces considerable overheads. In this section, a non-sequential mapping for linear lists is introduced which overcomes these problems.

The solution is to use a non-sequential mapping from a linear list onto a vector by means of a *linked list*. In essence, an extra layer is added to the mapping, as shown in Figure 7.8.

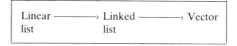

Figure 7.8

Each element in a linked list structure is called a *node*, and in addition to data each node contains a pointer field which points to the next node in the list. The pointer field of the last node contains a special end-of-list marker. A special head pointer must be maintained pointing to the first node, or *head*, of the linked list. When the head pointer contains the end-of-list marker, the list is empty. A diagram of one such structure is given in Figure 7.9.

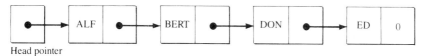

Figure 7.9

This is known as a *singly linked list* since each node has exactly one pointer to the next node.

The important feature of such a structure is that the nodes do not have to be stored in contiguous storage locations; the order of the list is maintained by the pointers. This greatly simplifies the insertion and deletion of items, and the sharing of common storage by several lists.

Consider the linked list in Figure 7.9. It represents four names in alphabetical order. Suppose that the name CHAS is to be added in its correct position. The required linked list is shown in Figure 7.10.

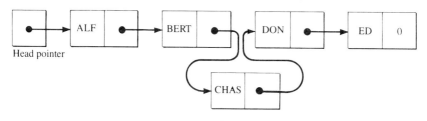

Figure 7.10

None of the original nodes needs to be moved. The actions needed to effect the insertion are

● Allocate a storage location to the new node
● Insert the new node's data field

- Find the required position of the new node in the existing list
- Insert the new node's pointer field
- Change the pointer field of the preceding node

Now suppose that the node containing BERT is to be deleted. The required linked list is shown in Figure 7.11.

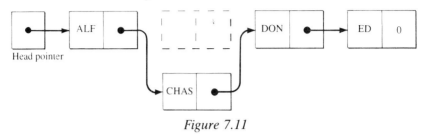

Head pointer

Figure 7.11

The actions needed to achieve this are

- Find the node to be deleted
- Change the pointer field of the preceding node
- Return the storage thus released to the set of unused storage

With both insertion and deletion operations, special care must be taken with regard to the empty list.

So far, the mapping from linear list to linked list has been considered. Now, the mapping from linked list to vector must be considered. In fact, two vectors are needed: one called DATA for the data field and one called LINK for the pointer field. The Ith node in the linked list is the combination of DATA [I] and LINK [I]. Choosing arbitrary locations for individual nodes, the linked list of Figure 7.10 could be represented by the vectors in Figure 7.12.

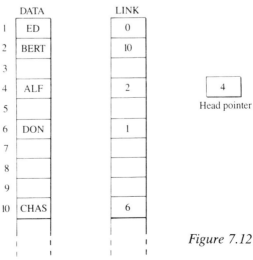

	DATA	LINK
1	ED	0
2	BERT	10
3		
4	ALF	2
5		
6	DON	1
7		
8		
9		
10	CHAS	6

4

Head pointer

Figure 7.12

Following the deletion of node BERT, the position would be as shown in Figure 7.13.

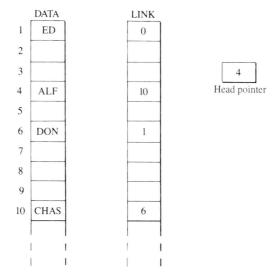

Figure 7.13

The linked list approach has greatly simplified the operations of insertion and deletion, at the expense of the extra storage involved, that is, the vector LINK. In general, the storage overhead on modern computers, with their large memories, is fully acceptable. Linked lists also facilitate the sharing of a storage structure by several linear lists. This can be illustrated by further consideration of the stack.

7.3.3 Stacks (onto linked lists)

It has been seen that representing several stacks in a single vector by a sequential mapping is prone to considerable data movement. Consider now the representation of several stacks by means of linked lists.

First, the problem of managing the free storage must be considered. When creating a new node, storage needs to be allocated quickly. Similarly, when deleting a node the released storage needs to be returned to the free storage so that it may be reused. The simplest approach is to treat the free storage itself as a linked list of unused nodes, usually called a *free list*. When an item is to be added to a stack, a node is taken from the free list. On deletion of an item from a stack, its node is added to the free list. Stack overflow occurs when the free list is empty.

Each stack is represented by a linked list. The top-of-stack pointer points to the head of the list, and all insertions and deletions are made at the head. Top-of-stack pointers are zero when the stack is empty. The bottom of the stack is the far end of the linked list. Consider the stack of Figure 7.2; its representation as a linked list is shown in Figure 7.14.

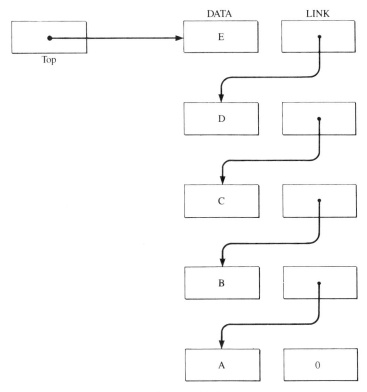

Figure 7.14

```
PROCEDURE INITIALISE (VAR LINKCOPY : LTYPE;
                      VAR STACKC1COPY,
                          STACK2COPY,
VAR I : STACKSIZE;          FREECOPY : POINTERTYPE);
BEGIN
        FOR I := 2 TO MAXSTACKSIZE DO
            LINKCOPY [I−1] := I;
        LINKCOPY [MAXSTACKSIZE] := 0;
        STACK1COPY := 0;
        STACK2COPY := 0;
        FREECOPY := 1
END (*INITIALISE*);
```

Figure 7.15

To initialise the storage area all the unused storage must be chained together into a free list. Also, a top-of-stack pointer must be set to zero for each stack to be used. Finally, a pointer to the head of the free list is needed; assume that this pointer is called FREE. Consider the following Pascal definition:

TYPE

.
.
.
.

STACKSIZE = 1 .. MAXSTACKSIZE;
POINTERTYPE = 0 .. MAXSTACKSIZE;
LTYPE = ARRAY [STACKSIZE] OF LITEM;
DTYPE = ARRAY [STACKSIZE] OF DITEM;
VAR

STACK1, STACK2, FREE : POINTERTYPE;
LINK   : LTYPE;
DATA : DTYPE;

where LITEM and DITEM are types defining the contents of the link field and the contents of the data field respectively in each node, and MAXSTACKSIZE is a constant defining the maximum number of nodes available. Figure 7.15 contains a procedure for the initialisation of a storage area in which two stacks will be maintained.

```
PROCEDURE PUSHITEM (ITEMCOPY : DITEM;
                    VAR STACK, FREECOPY : POINTERTYPE;
                    VAR LINKCOPY : LTYPE;
                    VAR DATACOPY : DTYPE);
VAR TEMPFREE : POINTERTYPE;
BEGIN
        IF FREECOPY = 0 THEN
            STACKOVERFLOW
        ELSE
        BEGIN
            (*Allocate storage for new node *)
            TEMPFREE := FREECOPY;
            FREECOPY := LINKCOPY [FREECOPY];
            (*Insert fields into new node *)
            DATACOPY[TEMPFREE] := ITEMCOPY;
            LINKCOPY[TEMPFREE] := STACK;
            (*Update stack pointer *)
            STACK := TEMPFREE
        END
END (*PUSHITEM*);
```

Figure 7.16

A typical call would be

INITIALISE (LINK, STACK1, STACK2, FREE);

Figure 7.16 contains a Pascal procedure to push an item DATAITEM onto one of the stacks.

To push an item onto STACK1, a suitable call would be

PUSHITEM (DATAITEM, STACK1, FREE, LINK, DATA);

To push an item onto STACK2, a suitable call would be

PUSHITEM (DATAITEM, STACK2, FREE, LINK, DATA);

Figure 7.17 contains the corresponding procedure to pop an item from one of the stacks.

```
PROCEDURE POPITEM (VAR ITEMCOPY : DITEM;
                   VAR STACK, FREECOPY : POINTERTYPE;
                   VAR LINKCOPY : LTYPE;
                   VAR DATACOPY : DTYPE);
VAR TEMPLINK : POINTERTYPE;
BEGIN
        IF STACK = 0 THEN
                STACKUNDERFLOW
        ELSE
        BEGIN
                (* Extract data field from node *)
                ITEMCOPY := DATACOPY [STACK];
                (* Return storage to free list *)
                TEMPLINK := LINKCOPY [STACK];
                LINKCOPY [STACK] := FREECOPY;
                FREECOPY := STACK;
                (* Update stack pointer *)
                STACK := TEMPLINK
        END
END (*POPITEM*) DITEM
```

Figure 7.17

To pop an item from STACK1, a suitable call would be

POPITEM (DATAITEM, STACK1, FREE, LINK, DATA);

To pop an item from STACK2, a suitable call would be

POPITEM (DATAITEM, STACK2, FREE, LINK, DATA);

With a minor modification to the initialise procedure, these three procedures are capable of maintaining any number of stacks in shared linked
storage.

7.3.4 Queues (onto vectors)

A *queue* is a linear list containing items that may be added at one end only,
the *rear*, and deleted at the other end only, the *front*. A queue is sometimes
referred to as a First In First Out (FIFO) list. Figure 7.18 shows the situation
diagrammatically.

Figure 7.18

Inserting the items A, B, C, D, E in that order into a queue and then
removing them would cause them to reappear in the same order A, B, C,
D, E.

The representation of a queue by means of a sequential mapping onto
a vector is possible but not simple. Consider the following Pascal definitions:

TYPE

.
.
.

.

       QSIZE = 1 .. MAXQSIZE;
       QPOINTER = 0 .. MAXQSIZE;
       QTYPE = ARRAY [QSIZE] OF ITEMS;
VAR
       FRONT, REAR : QPOINTER;
       QUEUE : QTYPE;

where ITEMS is a type defining the contents of each queue item and
MAXQSIZE is a constant defining the maximum number of items in the
queue. The rear pointer REAR always points to the last item in the queue.
The front pointer FRONT, however, always points to the empty item to
the left of the actual front of the queue. A queue of three items, stored
within a vector QUEUE, is shown in Figure 7.19.

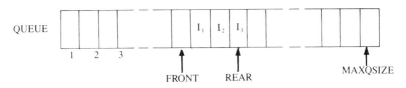

Figure 7.19

Using these conventions, the empty queue is indicated by FRONT = REAR, and the queue is initialised by setting both FRONT and REAR to zero.

Figure 7.20 shows a Pascal procedure to add new item to the queue.

```
PROCEDURE ADDTOQ (ITEMCOPY : ITEMS;
                  VAR Q : QTYPE;
                  VAR REARCOPY : QPOINTER);
BEGIN
      IF REARCOPY = MAXQSIZE THEN
              QOVERFLOW
      ELSE
      BEGIN
              REARCOPY := REARCOPY + 1;
              Q (REARCOPY) := ITEMCOPY
      END
END (*ADDTOQ*)
```

Figure 7.20

To add an item DATAITEM to the queue, a suitable call would be

ADDTOQ (DATAITEM, QUEUE, REAR);

Figure 7.21 shows a Pascal procedure to remove an item from the queue.

A typical call to remove an item from the queue and place it in DATAITEM would be

TAKEFROMQ (DATAITEM, QUEUE, REAR, FRONT);

This approach to the implementation of a queue has one major problem. Since items are added to one end and deleted from the other, the queue will move along the vector and eventually reach the end. Consider the situation shown in Figure 7.22.

```
PROCEDURE TAKEFROMQ (VAR ITEMCOPY : ITEMS;
                     VAR Q : QTYPE;
                     REARCOPY : QPOINTER;
                     VAR FRONTCOPY : QPOINTER);
BEGIN
    IF FRONTCOPY = REARCOPY THEN
        QUNDERFLOW
    ELSE
    BEGIN
        FRONTCOPY := FRONTCOPY + 1;
        ITEMCOPY := Q (FRONTCOPY)
    END
END (*TAKEFROMQ*)
```

Figure 7.21

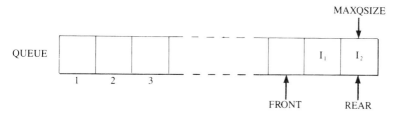

Figure 7.22

Any attempt to add another item to the queue will result in the procedure QOVERFLOW being called, even though the vector contains plenty of unused space. One solution to this is to move the queue to the other end of the vector and reset the FRONT and REAR pointers. This could be very time-consuming; a better solution is to treat the storage vector as if it were circular, as shown in Figure 7.23 (where M = MAXQSIZE).

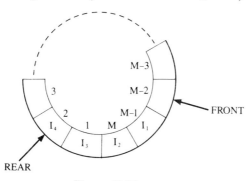

Figure 7.23

Several changes must be made to the procedures of Figures 7.20 and 7.21. First, when the pointer FRONT is incremented, it must be done by the following code.

```
IF FRONT = MAXQSIZE THEN
    FRONT := 1
ELSE
    FRONT := FRONT + 1;
```

The pointer REAR must be incremented in a similar way. Second, how to interpret FRONT = REAR must be decided. Does it mean that FRONT has caught up with REAR (queue empty) or that REAR has caught up with FRONT (queue full)? To avoid the ambiguity, define that FRONT = REAR means that the queue is empty and rewrite the ADDTOQ procedure in such a way that it never fills the last empty element in the vector. In other words, the queue is full when FRONT is one position clockwise from REAR. To initialise the queue, FRONT and REAR would be set to the same value, say 1.

The revised algorithms ADDTOQ and TAKEFROMQ should now be fairly easy to write, and are left as an exercise. See Exercise 7.8.6.

Under a sequential mapping onto a vector, it is impractical for two or more queues to share the same vector. Depending upon the frequency of additions and deletions, the queues would progress at different rates along the vector. If each queue is allocated to its own vector, then each vector must be large enough to accommodate the maximum possible size for its queue. Inevitably, this leads to wasted storage. In order for several queues to share the same storage structure, a non-sequential mapping via a linked list should be used.

7.3.5 Queues (onto linked lists)

A queue may be mapped in a very obvious way onto a linked list, as shown in Figure 7.24.

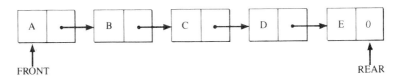

Figure 7.24

The direction of the pointers is important: if they are not from FRONT to REAR it is impossible to delete items from the front of the queue. In a linked list representation, FRONT must point to the first item in the queue. FRONT = 0 means that the queue is empty.

Consider the case of two queues sharing the same storage area, illustrated by the following Pascal definitions:

TYPE

.
.
.
.

```
QSIZE = 1 .. MAXQSIZE;
QPOINTER = 0 .. MAXQSIZE;
LTYPE = ARRAY [QSIZE] OF LITEM;
DTYPE = ARRAY [QSIZE] OF DITEM;
```
VAR
```
    FRONT1, REAR1,
    FRONT2, REAR2,
    FREE              : QPOINTER;
    LINK              : LTYPE;
    DATA              : DTYPE;
```

where LITEM and DITEM are types defining respectively the contents of the link field and the contents of the data field of each node, and MAXQSIZE is a constant defining the maximum number of nodes available. Figure 7.25 contains a procedure for the initialisation of the storage area and the two queues.

```
PROCEDURE INITIALISE (VAR LINKCOPY : LTYPE;
                      VAR FRONT1COPY,
                          FRONT2COPY,
                          FREECOPY : QPOINTER);
VAR I : QSIZE;
BEGIN
     FOR I := 2 TO MAXQSIZE DO
         LINKCOPY [I-1] := I;
     LINKCOPY [MAXQSIZE] := 0;
     FRONT1COPY := 0;
     FRONT2COPY := 0;
     FREECOPY := 1
END (*INITIALISE*)
```

Figure 7.25

A typical call would be

INITIALISE (LINK, FRONT1, FRONT2, FREE);

Figure 7.26 contains a procedure to add an item to one of the stacks.

```
PROCEDURE ADDTO1Q (ITEMCOPY : DITEM;
                   VAR FRONT, REAR, FREECOPY : QPOINTER
                   VAR LINKCOPY   : LTYPE;
                   VAR DATACOPY : DTYPE);
VAR TEMPFREE : QPOINTER;
BEGIN
       IF FREECOPY = 0 THEN
             QOVERFLOW
       ELSE
       BEGIN
             (*Allocate storage for new node *)
             TEMPFREE := FRECOPY;
             FREECOPY := LINKCOPY [FREECOPY];
             (*Insert fields into new node *)
             DATACOPY [TEMPFREE] := ITEMCOPY;
             LINKCOPY [TEMPFREE] := 0;
             IF FRONT = 0 THEN
             BEGIN
             (*Queue is empty *)
                   FRONT := TEMPFREE;
                   REAR  := TEMPFREE
             END
             ELSE
             BEGIN
             (*Queue not empty *)
                   LINKCOPY[REAR] := TEMPFREE;
                   REAR := TEMPFREE
             END
       END
END (*ADDTO1Q*)
```

Figure 7.26

To add an item to queue 1, a suitable call would be

ADDTO1Q (DATAITEM, FRONT1, REAR1, FREE, LINK, DATA);

To add an item to queue 2, a suitable call would be

ADDTO1Q (DATAITEM, FRONT2, REAR2, FREE, LINK, DATA);

Figure 7.27 contains the corresponding procedure to remove an item from one of the queues.

```
PROCEDURE TAKE FROM1Q (VAR ITEMCOPY : DITEM;
                          VAR FRONT, FREECOPY : QPOINTER;
                          VAR LINKCOPY  : LTYPE;
                          VAR DATACOPY : DTYPE);
VAR TEMPLINK : QPOINTER;
BEGIN
        IF FRONT = 0 THEN
            QUNDERFLOW
        ELSE
        BEGIN
            (* Extract data field from node *)
            ITEMCOPY := DATACOPY [FRONT];
            (* Return storage to free list *)
            TEMPLINK := LINKCOPY [FRONT];
            LINKCOPY [FRONT] := FREECOPY;
            FREECOPY := FRONT;
            (* Update queue pointer *)
            FRONT := TEMPLINK
        END
END (*TAKEFROM1Q*)
```

Figure 7.27

To take an item from queue 1 and place the data field in DATAITEM, a
suitable call would be

  TAKEFROM1Q (DATAITEM, FRONT1, FREE, LINK, DATA);

To take an item from queue 2 and place the data field in DATAITEM, a
suitable call would be

  TAKEFROM1Q (DATAITEM, FRONT2, FREE, LINK, DATA);

7.4 Trees

A full treatment of the tree data structure is beyond the scope of this book.
This section will introduce the general concepts of trees, and then present
one example of the use of a particular kind of tree.

A *tree* is a structure containing one or more nodes such that

● There is a specially designated node called the *root* of the tree
● Attached to the node there are zero or more subordinate nodes
● Each subordinate node is itself the root of a tree

This is a *recursive definition*. Part of the definition (the last part in the above
case) refers us back to the definition of the whole structure. A recursive

definition is the most convenient way of defining a tree. We shall see later that recursive procedures are an appropriate way of processing a tree.

Figure 7.28 contains an example of a tree describing the organisational structure of a fictitious college.

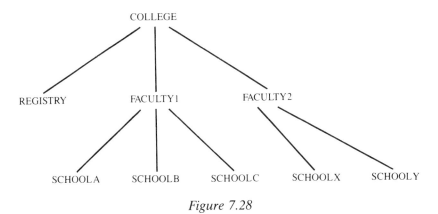

Figure 7.28

The node COLLEGE is the root node. Diagrams of trees are normally drawn with the root at the top. Nodes which have no subordinate nodes, for example, REGISTRY, SCHOOLA, etc., are called *leaf nodes*.

Representing a general tree in memory is not simple. Apart from its data field, each node must have a pointer field to each of its subtrees. Since the number of subtrees varies from one node to another, it follows that the storage required for a node will also vary. This causes problems in storage allocation, and also in the procedures for manipulating trees. The situation is simplified considerably if a restricted form of tree is considered: the binary tree.

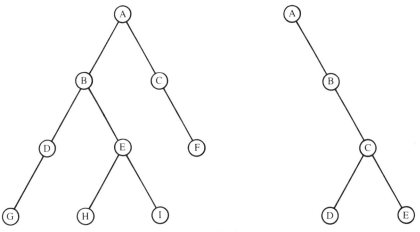

Figure 7.29

7.4.1 Binary trees

A *binary tree* is a tree-like structure where each node can have, at most, two subordinate nodes. The subordinate nodes are ordered: the first one being the root of the *left subtree* and the second one being the root of the *right subtree*. Figure 7.29 shows two examples of binary trees.

The number of subordinate nodes is always 0, 1 or 2.

The representation of a binary tree can be conveniently achieved by a linked list structure, where each node has the following contents:

LLINK	DATA	RLINK

LLINK and RLINK point to the root nodes of the left and right subtrees respectively.

Extending the approach used for linked stacks and linked queues, three separate storage vectors could be used: one for the LLINK fields, one for the DATA fields and one for the RLINK fields. A free list must still be maintained, but this does not need to be held as a binary tree; a simple linear list will still suffice. The free list can be chained together using either pointer field in each node, it does not matter which.

Consider the following Pascal definitions:

```
TYPE
        .
        .
        .
        .
        TREESIZE  = 1..MAXTREESIZE;
        TREELINK  = 0..MAXTREESIZE;
        LINKTYPE  = ARRAY [TREESIZE] OF LINKITEM;
        DATATYPE  = ARRAY [TREESIZE] OF DATAITEM;
VAR
        ROOT, FREE : TREELINK;
        LLINK, RLINK : LINKTYPE;
        DATA : DATATYPE;
```

where LINKITEM and DATAITEM are types defining respectively the contents of the link fields in each node and the contents of the data field in each node, and MAXTREESIZE is a constant defining the maximum number of nodes available. ROOT points to the root node of a tree, and is zero if the tree is empty. The LLINK field will be chosen to hold the chain of pointers for the free list. It should be noted that this method of handling the free storage allows deleted tree nodes to be returned to the free storage for subsequent reuse. Not all applications will require this facility.

Figure 7.30 contains a procedure for the initialisation of a storage area in which a binary tree will be maintained.

```
PROCEDURE INITIALISE (VAR LLINKCOPY : LINKTYPE;
                      VAR ROOTCOPY, FREECOPY : TREELINK);
VAR I : TREESIZE;
BEGIN
      FOR I := 2 TO MAXTREESIZE DO
          LLINKCOPY [I−1] := I;
      LLINKCOPY [MAXTREESIZE] := 0;
      ROOTCOPY := 0;
      FREECOPY := 1
END (*INITIALISE*)
```

Figure 7.30

A typical call would be

INITIALISE (LLINK, ROOT, FREE);

One use to which binary trees are commonly put is sorting. Randomly ordered items are inserted into a binary tree according to an ordering rule. The tree is then scanned and the items are extracted in sorted order.

Consider first the insertion phase. The ordering rule controlling insertion is that, for every node, all of the items inserted into its left subtree must be less than the node and all of the items inserted into its right subtree must be greater than the node. This assumes, of course, that all of the items are unique, but the extension to handle non-unique items is not difficult. Consider the letters E, C, A, D, F, B being inserted, in that order, into a binary tree. Figure 7.31 shows the stages of growth of the tree.

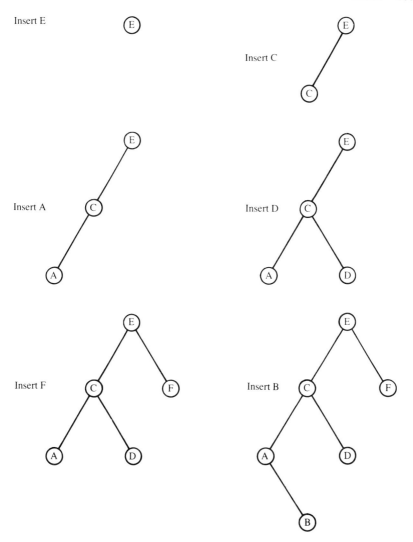

Figure 7.31

The algorithm to perform this insertion can be written in several ways. One of the neatest ways is based on the fact that the definition of a tree is recursive, that is, that each node is itself the root of another tree. A recursive procedure, that is, a procedure which calls itself, is shown in Figure 7.32.

```
PROCEDURE ADDTOSORTTREE (ITEMCOPY : DATAITEM;
                         VAR NODE, FREECOPY : TREELINK;
                         VAR LLINKCOPY, RLINKCOPY : LINKTYPE;
                         VAR DATACOPY : DATATYPE);
BEGIN
      IF NODE = 0 THEN
      BEGIN
      (* Leaf node found *)
          (*Allocate storage for new node *)
          NODE := FREECOPY;
          FREECOPY := LLINKCOPY [FREECOPY];
          (*Insert fields into new node *)
          DATACOPY [NODE] := ITEMCOPY;
          LLINKCOPY [NODE] := 0;
          RLINKCOPY [NODE] := 0
      END
      ELSE
      BEGIN
      (* Leaf node not yet found *)
          IF ITEMCOPY < DATACOPY [NODE] THEN
          (*Follow left subtree *)
              ADDTOSORTTREE (ITEMCOPY, LLINKCOPY [NODE],
                             FREECOPY, LLINKCOPY,
                             RLINKCOPY, DATACOPY)
          ELSE
          (*Follow right subtree *)
              ADDTOSORTTREE (ITEMCOPY, RLINKCOPY [NODE],
                             FREECOPY, LLINKCOPY,
                             RLINKCOPY, DATACOPY)
      END
END (*ADDTOSORTTREE*)
```

Figure 7.32

To insert the item DATAITEM into its correct position in the tree, a suitable call would be

ADDTOSORTTREE (DATAITEM, ROOT, FREE, LLINK, RLINK, DATA);

When all of the items have been inserted into the tree, phase 2 can commence. This involves scanning the tree and extracting the data field from each node. The way in which the tree is scanned must ensure that, for every node, data fields are extracted in the following order:

(1) All the nodes of the left subtree
(2) The node itself
(3) All the nodes of the right subtree

Once again, the best approach is to use a recursive procedure, as shown in Figure 7.33.

```
SCANSORTTREE (NODE : TREELINK;
                VAR LLINKCOPY, RLINKCOPY : LINKTYPE;
                VAR DATACOPY : DATATYPE);
BEGIN
        IF NODE < > 0 THEN
        BEGIN
                (* Follow pointer to left subtree *)
                SCANSORTTREE (LLINKCOPY [NODE], LLINKCOPY,
                        RLINKCOPY, DATACOPY);
                (* Output data field of node *)
                WRITELN (DATACOPY [NODE]);
                (* Follow pointer to right subtree *)
                SCANSORTTREE (RLINKCOPY [NODE], LLINKCOPY,
                        RLINKCOPY,DATACOPY)
        END
END (*SCANSORTTREE*)
```

Figure 7.33

All the nodes are output in sorted order by the single call

SCANSORTTREE (ROOT, LLINK, RLINK, DATA);

Scanning the nodes of a tree in some predetermined manner is known as a *tree-walk* or *tree-traversal*. With reference to binary trees, three different types of tree-traversal are commonly used. Each type relates to the order in which the nodes are processed, or 'visited'.

● *Pre-order tree-traversal.* The nodes are visited in the order
  (1) The node itself
  (2) All the nodes of the left subtree
  (3) All the nodes of the right subtree
● *In-order tree-traversal.* The nodes are visited in the order
  (1) All the nodes of the left subtree
  (2) The node itself
  (3) All the nodes of the right subtree
● *End-order tree-traversal.* The nodes are visited in the order
  (1) All the nodes of the left subtree
  (2) All the nodes of the right subtree
  (3) The node itself

The tree-traversal of Figure 7.33 is an example of in-order tree-traversal. Unfortunately, the names given above for the three types of tree-traversal have not been used consistently by different authors. In some cases, they have not been used consistently by the same author! Just to add to the confusion, the name *post-order traversal* has been used variously to describe both in-order and end-order tree-traversals. Great care must be taken when interpreting these names.

7.5 Records

So far, homogeneous data structures have been considered, that is, structures having elements of the same type. A *record* is a collection of elements which may be of different types. Each element of a record is called a *field*.

A record is used to group together all the information about a particular object. For example, associated with each employee of a company would be a record containing all the information needed to produce a pay-slip: name, department code, tax code, hours worked, and hourly rate.

In Pascal, this might be written as the following type definition.

```
TYPE
     EMPLOYEEDETAILS =
     RECORD
            NAME : PACKED ARRAY [1 . . 20] OF CHAR;
            DEPTCODE : PACKED ARRAY [1 . . 4] OF CHAR;
            TAXCODE : 1 . . 999;
            HOURS : 0 . . 60;
            RATE : REAL
     END;
```

Variables of this type can then be declared, for example

```
VAR
     TEMPCOPY : EMPLOYEEDETAILS;
     PAYROLL : ARRAY [1 . . 100] OF EMPLOYEEDETAILS;
```

Individual fields can then be accessed as

```
TEMPCOPY.NAME
PAYROLL [1].TAXCODE
            etc.
```

Allowing for incompatibilities between the languages, the COBOL equivalent of the above record definition could be written as follows:

```
01   EMPLOYEEDETAILS.
        03   NAME            PIC X (20).
        03   DEPTCODE        PIC X (4).
        03   TAXCODE         PIC 999.
        03   HOURS           PIC 99.
        03   RATE            PIC 99V99.
```

The record in Pascal should be thought of as simply another data type. The fields which make up a record can themselves be of any data type: for example, INTEGER, ARRAY, even RECORD. This allows the Pascal programmer to define very complex data structures.

The record in COBOL has a specific function: it is the unit of data that is input or output at any one time. The READ and WRITE statements in COBOL operate on records, and records are always defined at the 01-level. The items subordinate to the record enable the programmer to access individual fields.

The record in Pascal may also be used as the unit of input/output, but its use is not restricted to this.

7.6 Files

A *file* is a collection of records. It is, therefore, the conglomeration of information about similar objects. For example, a file used as input to a payroll program would contain one record per employee. In Pascal, it could be defined simply as

```
VAR
        PAYROLL : FILE OF EMPLOYEEDETAILS;
```

The way in which a file is processed will vary from one application to another. Consider the example of a payroll program. In order to produce the pay-slips, each record must be processed in turn, starting with the first, proceeding through the file and finishing with the last. Now consider a file containing details of stock levels for items in a warehouse. An enquiry about a particular item will require access to the record for that item. Records will be accessed in random order, and many records will not be accessed at all. To cater for the requirements of different applications, computer systems provide a variety of file structures.

The simplest type of file is the *serial file*, in which records are read and written serially. The records of a serial file are written to consecutive locations on the hardware device. The physical characteristics of devices such as magnetic tapes and printers enforce this consecutive allocation, but it can also be used for serial files on disc. The use of consecutive allocation allows very efficient use to be made of the storage available. However, it is not possible to access a particular record of a serial file without first having accessed all its predecessors. This restriction causes no problems for the pay-slips program.

A serial file in which records are ordered according to the value of one of the fields is called an *ordered serial file* or a *sequential file*. These are particularly useful when a program uses two or more files and the processing is simplified if the files are in a similar order. Consider again the payroll file. Suppose that there is also an update file containing details of required changes, for example, the insertion of a new employee record or the alteration of an employee's tax code. The changes could be made most efficiently if the payroll and update files were both in order of, for example, employee name. As far as the programmer is concerned, sequential files must still be processed record by record from the beginning. From the system's point of view, they are not as efficient as serial files since insertions and deletions can upset the underlying serial organisation.

Both serial and sequential files are inappropriate for handling enquiries in the warehouse stock example. It must be possible to access an individual record directly, perhaps by quoting a unique item code. Computer manufacturers offer a variety of direct access file structures, and there is a lack of uniformity between them. Two of the most common types are *indexed sequential files* and *hashed random files*. Both offer considerable flexibility to the applications programmer, but both make relatively inefficient use of the storage available.

Pascal offers only serial files. Full versions of COBOL offer all types. Refer to your specialist language texts for details.

7.7 Summary

This chapter has introduced some more advanced data structures. Ways of implementing them have been examined, and it has been shown that several levels of mapping are sometimes required between logical data structure and physical data structure.

The associated algorithms have been presented in Pascal, but it should not be assumed that COBOL is inappropriate for manipulating data structures. With the exception of the recursive procedures associated with trees, all the algorithms can be rewritten easily in COBOL, and you are strongly recommended to do so with at least some of them.

The most important feature of this chapter has been the introduction of linked structures. The implementations of stacks, queues and trees are merely examples of the uses to which linked structures can be put. Structures where each node has a number of linking fields can be used to describe the most complex situations, and they have great value in programming and computing in general.

7.8 Exercises

7.8.1   Code the Pascal Boolean function STACKNOTEMPTY which is true if a stack is not empty and false otherwise. See Section 7.3.1.

7.8.2   Code the Pascal procedure POPASTACK which corresponds to PUSHASTACK in Figure 7.6.

7.8.3   Write a Pascal program which uses a stack to test if a string of characters is a palindrome.

7.8.4   Write a Pascal program which inputs positive and negative integers, terminated by a zero, and prints out first the positive integers and then the negative integers in the reverse order to their input.

7.8.5   Dry run the procedures of Figure 7.15, 7.16 and 7.17 and observe their behaviour.

7.8.6   Write procedures ADDTOQ and TAKEFROMQ for a queue held in a 'circular' vector.

7.8.7   Write a program to read in 20 10-character names and store them in a linked list. Then read in some more names and, for each, indicate whether or not it is in the list, deleting it if it is. Finally, print out the resulting list.

7.8.8   Write a program which reads randomly ordered 10-character names, stores them in a sort tree, and then outputs them in ascending order.

7.8.9   Modify Figure 7.33 to produce recursive Pascal procedures to perform
● Pre-order tree-traversal
● End-order tree-traversal

CHAPTER 8

Program implementation problems and solutions

8.1 Introduction □ 8.2 Structure clashes □ 8.3 Program inversion □ 8.4 Recognition problems □ 8.5 Summary □ 8.6 Exercise

8.1 Introduction

In Chapter 6, the JSP method for designing structured programs was introduced by means of an extended example, chosen to illustrate the application of the basic technique. However, not all examples are so well behaved, and the basic JSP method has to be extended to deal with the more complicated cases. In this chapter, some of the problems commonly encountered in the design of structured programs will be considered and, again by means of examples, some suitable solutions will be examined. Specifically, structure clashes and recognition problems will be dealt with. This chapter provides only an introductory treatment of these two problem areas, but should adequately cater for the needs of a trainee programmer. Specialist books should be consulted for a detailed treatment.

8.2 Structure clashes

The fundamental objective of the JSP method is to base the program's structure on the structure of the data being processed. This involves identifying correspondences between components of the input data and components of the output data. For a correspondence to exist it is necessary that the components occur

● The same number of times
● In the same order

If it is not possible to identify a correspondence between related components in the two data structures, then it is likely that a *structure clash* exists. The fact that structure clashes sometimes occur is not evidence of a weakness in the JSP method; structure clashes occur where there is an underlying difficulty in the problem being investigated.

It is possible to classify structure clashes into two types: order clashes and boundary clashes.

8.2.1 Order clashes

It is common for the lowest level component of the input data structure to be related to the lowest level component of the output data structure. Where it is not possible to identify a formal correspondence between two such components because they occur in a different order, then an *order clash* has occurred.

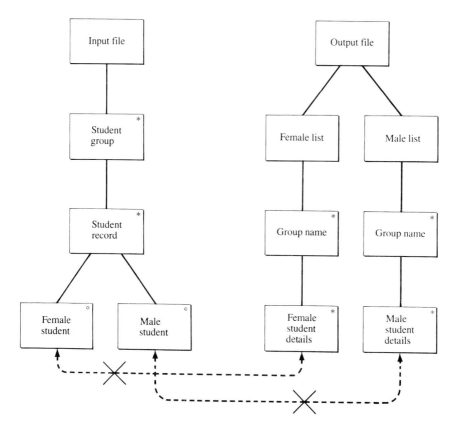

Figure 8.1

Example 8.1

Consider a file of records containing student details, one record per student. The records are organised into student groups, and within each group the records appear in alphabetic order of student name. An output file is to contain a list of female students and a list of male students. Within each list, student names are to appear under their group identifier. The data structures for the inp·¹t and output files are shown in Figure 8.1.

Each record in the input file produces one record in the output file. However, it is not possible to identify correspondences since the records are not in the same order in the two files.

In this particular problem, it is very easy to resolve the structure clash. The clash is caused by different orderings of the data; therefore, the solution is to re-order the input data so that it corresponds to the required output data. The input data should be sorted using

● The male/female indicator as the primary key
● The group name as the secondary key
● The student name as the tertiary key

It will then be easy to produce the required output from the resorted file.

In essence, the original problem has been solved by using two programs: the first uses the original data to produce an *intermediate file*, and the second uses the intermediate file to produce the required results. This mechanism is shown in Figure 8.2.

Figure 8.2

It should be noted that there are other ways to solve this particular problem. For instance, if it is possible to read the entire file twice, the female students could be extracted on the first pass and the male students could be extracted on the second. Alternatively, if sufficient main memory space was available, the entire file could be read into a table which could then be accessed directly to yield the information in the required order. In general, these two approaches are not as practical as the intermediate file approach, particularly where very large input files are concerned.

8.2.2 Boundary clashes

Boundary clashes are normally associated with data structures where

● The size of a component may vary
● The number of repetitions of a subcomponent within a component may vary
● Both the above

Boundary clashes are often found in programs which produce reports, where the physical characteristics of the reporting medium, such as the length of a page, must be taken into account. Consider the following problem frequently faced by a word processing package.

Example 8.2

An input file contains a number of records of unpredictable length. Each input record contains text consisting of a number of words separated by spaces. Without splitting a word over two lines, it is required to print the text on a listing device whose line length, specified as a number of characters, is supplied as a parameter to the program.

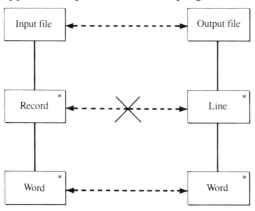

Figure 8.3

   This problem is typical of a word processor having to reformat stored text when new margins have been specified. The input and output data structures are given in Figure 8.3.

An obvious correspondence exists at the highest level since the text of the output file consists precisely of the text of the input file. Similarly, a correspondence exists at the lowest level, since the same words in the same order appear in both files. When an attempt to establish a correspondence at the intermediate level is made, the structure clash is encountered. This boundary clash is so called because it is caused by end-of-record boundaries not corresponding to end-of-line boundaries. It is not possible to say whether a record consists of a number of lines, or a line consists of a number of records.

   Again, the solution is to split the problem into two programs and introduce an intermediate file. This intermediate file must be designed very carefully to have correspondences with both the input file and the output file. In practice, it is best to define the intermediate file in terms of low-level components which are common to both. In this example, the obvious candidate is the word. Figure 8.4 shows the structure of the intermediate file and its correspondences with the input and output files.

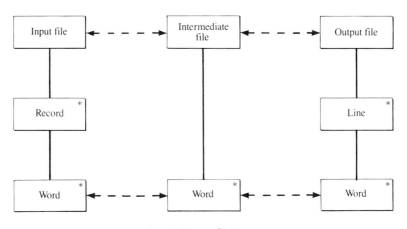

Figure 8.4

With the intermediate file simply organised as an iteration of words, the outline structures of the two required programs become obvious. They are shown in Figure 8.5.

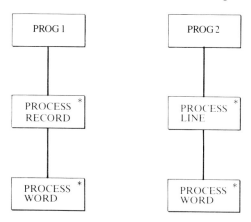

Figure 8.5

8.3 Program inversion

The above Sections 8.2.1 and 8.2.2 show how two types of structure clash may be resolved by introducing an intermediate file and using two programs to solve the original problem. In complex situations, it may be necessary to introduce more than one intermediate file and split the solution across several independent programs, as shown in Figure 8.6.

Structure clashes can always be resolved by using this intermediate file method. This approach, however, is usually quite expensive, both in terms of the storage space required for the extra file and in terms of the time needed to perform all the extra input/output operations.

In some cases, the inherent nature of the problem forces the intermediate file approach to be adopted. These problems are often characterised by the need to process the data in a different order to that in the file. Such problems are known as *two pass problems*. The order clash of Example 8.1 is an example of a two pass problem.

In other cases, it is possible to avoid the use of the intermediate file and two programs. If one program is writing records sequentially to the intermediate file, and the other program is reading records sequentially from the same intermediate file, then the two programs can be combined by making one a subroutine of the other. The records can then be handed over individually and directly through the subroutine parameter passing mechanism, and there is no need for an intermediate file. Such problems are known as *one pass problems*. The boundary clash of Example 8.2 is an example of a one pass problem.

This technique is known as *program inversion*. It consists of designing a program as two subprograms using an intermediate file, but then coding

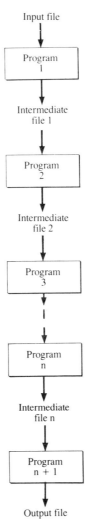

Figure 8.6

it as a main program and a subroutine with no intermediate file. When using program inversion, it is vital to design the program initially as if it were going to use an intermediate file. This stage must not be omitted. It ensures a clean separation of function between what eventually become the main program and subroutine.

In order to examine the mechanism of program inversion, and to appreciate the problems involved, Example 8.2 will again be considered. More detailed program structures for the two subprograms involved are shown in Figures 8.7 and 8.8.

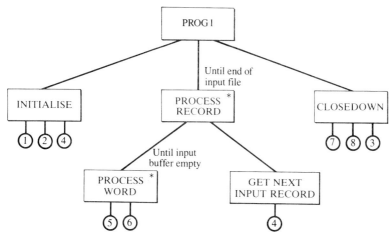

Action list

1. Open input file
2. Open intermediate file
3. Stop program
4. Read input record

5. Remove next word from input buffer
6. Write word to intermediate file
7. Close input file
8. Close intermediate file

Figure 8.7

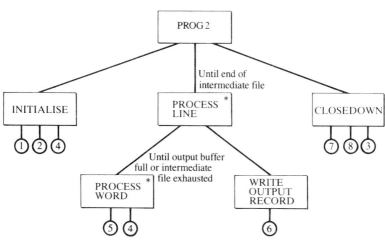

Action list

1. Open intermediate file
2. Open output file
3. Stop program
4. Read word from intermediate file

5. Place next word in output buffer
6. Write output record
7. Close intermediate file
8. Close output file

Figure 8.8

```
PROG1 seq
      Open input file
      Open intermediate file
      Read input record
      PROCESS-RECORD iter until end of input file
            PROCESS-WORD iter until input buffer empty
                  Remove next word from input buffer
                  Write word to intermediate file
            PROCESS-WORD end
            Read input record
      PROCESS-RECORD end
      Close input file
      Close intermediate file
PROG1 end
```

Figure 8.9

```
PROG2 seq
      Open intermediate file
      Open output file
      Read word from intermediate file
      PROCESS-LINE iter until end of intermediate file
            PROCESS-WORD iter until output buffer full
                              or end of intermediate file
                  Place next word in output buffer
                  Read word from intermediate file
            PROCESS-WORD end
            Write output record
      PROCESS-LINE end
      Close intermediate file
      Close output file
PROG2 end
```

Figure 8.10

The schematic logic derived from these structures is shown in Figures 8.9 and 8.10. The statements relating to the intermediate file have been printed in bold.

In combining the two programs all references to the intermediate file are removed and a subroutine calling and returning mechanism introduced. The points at which the main program and subroutine will pass control are the READ and WRITE statements which refer to the intermediate file.

Assume that PROG1 is the main program and PROG2 the subroutine. Every time PROG1 has a word ready to pass on, it must call PROG2. So every instruction which writes to the intermediate file must be replaced by a CALL instruction with the word as a parameter. Similarly, every instruction in PROG2 which reads from the intermediate file must be replaced by a return to PROG1 so that PROG1 may produce another word.

A problem arises because of the use of the read-ahead technique. In a program being inverted into a subroutine, there will be more than one READ statement. Each of these defines a different entry point to the subroutine, demanding a mechanism to ensure that when the main program calls back, the subroutine will resume processing from the point it had reached. The simplest way of achieving this is to number each return point and, just before leaving the subroutine, store the number of the return point to be used. On re-entry to the subroutine, the stored number is used to select the appropriate point to resume processing. In COBOL, this is easily achieved by use of a GO TO ... DEPENDING ON ... instruction, and the same mechanism can be employed in the schematic logic used here.

The necessary changes to the schematic logic of PROG1 and PROG2 are shown in Figures 8.11 and 8.12. Newly inserted instructions are printed in bold.

```
PROG1 seq
     Open input file
     ~~Open intermediate file~~
     Read input record
     PROCESS-RECORD iter until end of input file
          PROCESS-WORD iter until input buffer empty
               Remove next word from input buffer
               ~~Write word to intermediate file~~
               Call subroutine PROG2
          PROCESS-WORD end
          Read input record
     PROCESS-RECORD end
     Close input file
     ~~Close intermediate file~~
PROG1 end
```

Figure 8.11

Notice that the initial read-ahead in PROG2 is simply deleted. The original value of ENTRY-NO must be 1 so that the initial housekeeping, such as opening the output file, is carried out on the very first entry to the subroutine. The second and subsequent READ statements are replaced by a sequence of statements which stores the number of the return point and then exits from the subroutine. In general, the nth READ statement $n \geq 2$ is replaced by

> Move n To ENTRY-NO
> Go To PROG-EXIT
> ENTRY-n:

```
        PROG2 seq
            Go to ENTRY-1, ENTRY-2 depending on ENTRY-NO
    ENTRY-1:
                ~~Open intermediate file~~
                Open output file
                ~~Read word from intermediate file~~
                PROCESS-LINE iter until end of intermediate file
                    PROCESS-WORD iter until output buffer full
                                            or end of intermediate file
                        Place next word in output buffer
                        ~~Read word from intermediate file~~
                Move 2 to ENTRY-NO
                Go to PROG-EXIT
    ENTRY-2:
                PROCESS-WORD end
                Write output record
                PROCESS-LINE end
                ~~Close intermediate file~~
                Close output file
    PROG-EXIT:
            Exit
        PROG2 end
```

Figure 8.12

Assume that the maximum length of the input records and the output line is 100 characters. Also, assume that the maximum length of an individual word is 20 characters. The outline COBOL programs corresponding to the schematic logic are shown in Figures 8.13 and 8.14.

The program reading the intermediate file would have expected to find an end-of-file condition when the file was exhausted. The new PROG2 receives its data from PROG1, and so PROG1 must inform PROG2 when the end of data has been reached. This is the purpose of the second parameter in the subroutine call. The second CALL instruction near the end of PROG1 is needed to communicate the end-of-file condition to PROG2.

Note how the iteration constructs from the schematic logic have been implemented by means of IF and GO TO statements, rather than PERFORM statements. This is necessary in order to enable program inversion to be carried out. This systematic use of GO TO statements is perfectly acceptable in structured programming. Any unstructured use of the GO TO statement should be avoided.

The choice of PROG1 as the main program and PROG2 as the subroutine was purely arbitrary. It would have been equally feasible to invert PROG1

```
                .
                .
                .
        SELECT INPUT-FILE ASSIGN TO . . .
                .
                .
                .
                .
FILE  SECTION.
FD   IN-FILE
        DATA RECORD IS IN-REC.
01     IN-REC PIC X(100).
WORKING-STORAGE SECTION.
01     INT-REC-1 PIC X(20).
01     EOF-FLAG PIC 9 VALUE 0.
                .
                .
                .
                .
PROCEDURE DIVISION.
PROG1-SEQ.
        OPEN INPUT IN-FILE.
        READ IN-FILE, AT END MOVE 1 TO EOF-FLAG.
PROCESS-RECORD-ITER.
        IF  EOF-FLAG = 1 GO TO PROCESS-RECORD-END.
PROCESS-WORD-ITER.
        IF input buffer empty GO TO PROCESS-WORD-END.
                .
                .
                .
                .
        move next word from input buffer into INT-REC-1.
                .
                .
                .
                .
        CALL PROG2 USING INT-REC-1, EOF-FLAG.
        GO TO PROCESS-WORD-ITER.
PROCESS-WORD-END.
        READ IN-FILE, AT END MOVE 1 TO EOF-FLAG.
        GO TO PROCESS-RECORD-ITER.
PROCESS-RECORD-END.
        CLOSE INPUT-FILE.
        CALL PROG2 USING INT-REC-1, EOF-FLAG.
        STOP RUN.
```

Figure 8.13

```
            .
            .
            .
        SELECT OUT-FILE ASSIGN TO . . .
            .
            .
            .
    FILE SECTION.
    FD  OUT-FILE
        DATA RECORD IS OUT-REC.
    01  OUT-REC PIC X(100).
    WORKING-STORAGE SECTION.
    01  RETURN-NO PIC 9 VALUE 1.
            .
            .
            .
    LINKAGE SECTION.
    01  INT-REC-2 PIC X(20).
    01  END-FLAG PIC 9.
    PROCEDURE DIVISION USING INT-REC-2, END-FLAG.
    PROG2-SEQ.
        GO TO ENTRY-1, ENTRY-2 DEPENDING ON RETURN-NO.
    ENTRY-1.
        OPEN OUTPUT OUT-FILE.
    PROCESS-LINE-ITER.
        IF END-FLAG = 1 GO TO PROCESS-LINE-END.
    PROCESS-WORD-ITER.
        IF END-FLAG = 1 OR output buffer full
            GO TO PROCESS-WORD-END.
            .
            .
            .
        move INT-REC-2 into output buffer
            .
            .
            .
        MOVE 2 TO ENTRY-NO.
        GO TO PROG-EXIT.
    ENTRY-2.
        GO TO PROCESS-WORD-ITER.
    PROCESS-WORD-END.
        WRITE OUT-REC AFTER 1.
        GO TO PROCESS-LINE-ITER.
    PROCESS-LINE-END.
        CLOSE OUT-FILE.
    PROG-EXIT.
        EXIT PROGRAM.
```

Figure 8.14

and make it a subroutine of PROG2. Whenever PROG2 needed a word, it would call PROG1 to provide it; PROG1 would return the required word as a parameter.

The mechanism of program inversion illustrated in this section is based on the assumption that the implementation language is COBOL. When other languages are used, the general approach is the same but the detailed mechanism may differ.

8.4 Recognition problems

When execution reaches the evaluation of a condition, and some of the information required for the evaluation is not yet available, a *recognition problem* exists. The two principal ways of dealing with recognition problems are multiple read-ahead and backtracking.

8.4.1 Multiple read-ahead

In order to make available all the necessary information at the time a condition is evaluated, it is sometimes possible to extend the read-ahead technique to *multiple read-ahead*. This is particularly true where two or more consecutive records in a file contain information about the same logical entity. Consider Example 8.3.

Example 8.3

A file contains student details, two records per student. The first record contains personal details such as name, address, etc.; the second record contains the mark awarded in an end-of-year programming examination. A list is required of those students who failed programming together with the mark each achieved.

It is clear that in order to decide whether to print a student's name from the personal details record, access to the information on the succeeding record is needed. The solution is straightforward and involves reading two records at once, storing them safely in different buffer areas. The detailed program design is given in Figure 8.15.

The program structure implicitly assumes that the input file contains correct data. If this assumption cannot be made, then several defensive changes must be made to enable the program to cope with incorrect data. To be able to check that personal details records are correctly interspersed with examination mark records, it would be necessary to include a 'record type' field in each record. Also, a student identification number in every record would enable verification to be made that a particular examination mark

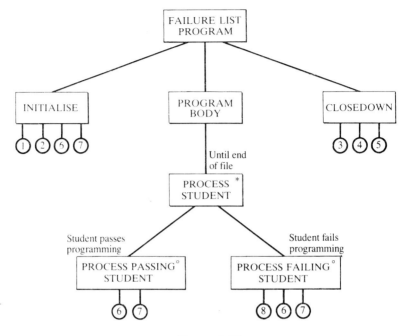

Figure 8.15

record did in fact relate to the immediately previous personal details record. If an erroneous data file contained an odd number of records, an attempt would be made to perform action 7 on an already exhausted file. In some languages this would have no harmful effect, but good programmers should always aim to avoid reading from an empty file.

The multiple read-ahead technique has been illustrated by means of an example involving two records. It is possible to extend the technique to cope with any number of records. Each additional record to be read ahead, however, will usually require an additional buffer area for its storage. This technique cannot be used if it is not possible to predict the number of records to be held in main memory.

8.4.2 Backtracking

A more general solution to recognition problems is provided by the *backtracking* technique. This technique can be used where multiple read-ahead is either inappropriate or unacceptably complex. As a simple example of the application of backtracking, consider Example 8.4.

Example 8.4

A file contains student details, one batch of consecutive records per student. The first record in a batch contains personal details such as name, address, etc. Following the personal details record, there is a variable number of subject records, each containing the subject name and the grade achieved. Personal details records are distinguishable from subject records. A list is required of those students who have passed all their subjects.

A detailed program structure is given in Figure 8.16.

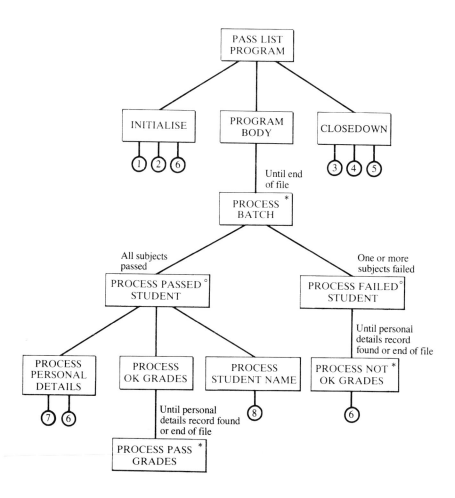

Figure 8.16

The corresponding schematic logic is shown in Figure 8.17.

```
PASS-LIST seq
   Open input file
   Open output file
   Read input record
   PROGRAM-BODY iter until end of file
      BATCH sel if all subjects passed
         PASS-STUDENT seq
            Store student name
            Read input record
            OK-GRADES iter until personal details record found
               Read input record
            OK-GRADES end
            Write student name
         PASS-STUDENT end
      BATCH or if one or more subjects failed
         FAIL-STUDENT seq
            NOT-OK-GRADES iter until personal details record found
               Read input record
            NOT-OK-GRADES end
         FAIL-STUDENT end
      BATCH end
   PROGRAM-BODY end
   Close input file
   Close output file
   Stop program
PASS-LIST end
```

Figure 8.17

The schematic logic of Figure 8.15 cannot be converted into programming code because it contains a recognition problem on entry to the component PROCESS BATCH. It must be determined whether all subjects are passed, and at that moment of execution not all the necessary information is available. The technique of backtracking involves making an assumption, or hypothesis, about the truth of the condition and going on to execute one of the alternative paths. If the hypothesis is subsequently found to be incorrect, the program must backtrack to the point where the original decision was made and begin executing the alternative path.

If a program has to backtrack, it is likely that some data will have been processed between making the original decision and discovering that the hypothesis was incorrect. In incorporating the backtracking into the program, the program designer must assess the effect of processing such data. It may have no effect on the required results, in which case it can be safely ignored. On the other hand, it may corrupt the required results, in which case the processing must somehow be undone. The handling of these *side effects* is a major problem with backtracking. The hypothesis made should be chosen to minimise side effects.

In Example 8.4, if it is assumed that all subjects have been passed, and then a failure is discovered, action 7 (store student name) will have been performed unnecessarily. However, this has no harmful effects on the required results. On the other hand, if it is assumed that all students have failed at least one subject, and then discovered that there is one who has passed them all, action 7 has not been performed and the student's name cannot, therefore, be printed. To minimise the side effects, it should be hypothesised, therefore, that all students have passed all of their subjects.

The next step is to amend the schematic logic which corresponds to the program component containing the recognition problem. BATCH *sel* is replaced by BATCH *posit*, producing the hypothesis that all examinations have been passed. The BATCH *or* at the head of the alternative path is replaced by BATCH *admit*. If, in processing the *posit* path, a failed subject is discovered, it is necessary to *quit* the *posit* path and begin executing the *admit* path, and so admit that the hypothesis was incorrect.

The amendments to the schematic logic are shown in Figure 8.18.

```
              .
              .
              .
              .
    BATCH posit
          PASS-STUDENT seq
                Store student name
                Read input record
                OK-GRADES iter until personal details record found
                      Read input record, quit BATCH posit if subject failed
                OK-GRADES end
                Write student name
          PASS-STUDENT end
    BATCH admit
          FAIL-STUDENT seq
              .
              .
              .
              .
```

Figure 8.18

Generally, the coding in the *admit* path may need to undo some of the side effects of the *posit* path. In this case it does not.

Note that the *admit* path is only entered from the *quit* construct. In Pascal and COBOL, the *quit* is most easily implemented by use of a GOTO statement. The COBOL PROCEDURE DIVISION code, equivalent to Figure 8.18, is given in Figure 8.19.

```
                .
                .
                .
    BATCH-POSIT.
            MOVE STUDENT-NAME TO STUDENT-NAME-COPY.
            READ INFILE, AT END MOVE 1 TO EOF-FLAG.
    OK-GRADES-ITER.
            IF RECORD-TYPE = PERSONAL GO TO OK-GRADES-END.
            READ INFILE, AT END MOVE 1 TO EOF-FLAG.
            IF SUBJECT-GRADE = FAIL GO TO BATCH-ADMIT.
            GO TO OK-GRADES-ITER.
    OK-GRADES-END.
            DISPLAY STUDENT-NAME-COPY.
            GO TO BATCH-END.
    BATCH-ADMIT.
                .
                .
                .
    BATCH-END.
                .
                .
                .
```

Figure 8.19

It was stated in Chapter 6 that one of the characteristics of a good program component was a single entry and a single exit. The *posit*, *quit*, *admit* construct produces multiple exit paths, but is usually better than alternative approaches to the solution of a recognition problem. Great care must be taken to ensure that GOTO statements are only used in this controlled way.

8.5 Summary

The JSP method of program design can most easily be applied to the processing of traditional files where the data is organised in a hierarchy. Where the file is not so conveniently organised, the JSP method is still appropriate, and can be adapted to deal with problems which are inherent in the data. This chapter has introduced some of these problems, and outlined suitable solutions. A specialist text on JSP is recommended for a detailed treatement.

8.6 Exercise

A file contains address details, one set per record. Each record contains four fields: NAME, STREET, TOWN and POSTCODE. A listing is required with each field appearing on a separate line, and two addresses appearing side by side on the page.

CHAPTER 9

Program documentation

9.1 Introduction □ 9.2 The purpose of documentation □ 9.3 The components of documentation □ 9.4 Documentation within the program listing □ 9.5 The provision of documentation □ 9.6 Summary

9.1 Introduction

If a programmer was asked to name which part of his job he least liked, the chances are that program documentation would be his answer. Writing out text and drawing diagrams to describe the program usually hold much less attraction than designing and coding the program. Since much of the final documentation is produced quite late in the program development cycle, it is largely a matter of describing what has already been done and consequently lacks a sense of creativity. Nevertheless, all programmers would admit, albeit grudgingly, that the production of program documentation is an important part of their job, and they would probably complain that they are not given enough time to do it properly.

This chapter describes the different types of documentation that may be produced, and discusses their importance in relation to their objectives.

9.2 The purpose of documentation

The purpose of documentation is to make a program understandable, easy to use and easy to maintain. It provides general and detailed information about the program. Before describing what should be included in a program's documentation, the needs that documentation is supposed to satisfy must be identified. The documentation must act as a reference for four different groups of people:

- Management
- Users
- Programmers
- Operators

These four groups of people require different types of information about a program. Some pieces of documentation will only be relevant to one or two of the groups. Other pieces of documentation may be relevant to all four groups but will be required to a different level of detail by each. For these reasons it is normal for each group to be presented with a different set of documentation, relevant to the requirements of the group and at a level of detail appropriate to the group.

9.2.1 Management documentation

Most programs are developed for use by commercial and industrial organisations. Unless the organisation is very small, the responsibility for program development will be vested in a computing department. The management of the organisation, and the management of the computing department, will not be interested in the detailed design of particular programs. What they will require is an overview of the new program, describing the functions performed by the program and identifying how it will affect the various departments within the organisation. This overview must be produced at the very beginning of the program life cycle, so that management can authorise the work.

Before the bulk of the work starts, management will also require an implementation schedule in order to monitor the progress of the work. This schedule will be of particular importance to the management of the computing department, who are responsible for assigning people to tasks and for identifying deadlines for individual tasks. A commonly-used technique is to establish *milestones* throughout the program life cycle. These are dates by which a clearly identified subset of tasks should be complete. The cost of a program being delivered late can be considerable, particularly if it is being written for an outside organisation. Every attempt should be made to recognise schedule slippage as soon as it occurs. An implementation schedule and the minutes of regular formal progress meetings form an essential part of management documentation.

9.2.2 User documentation

The user of a program is the person for whom the program is written. In fact, most programs are not written for a single user; they are used by many people who all need to perform the same task. The user of a program is most unlikely to be the programmer who wrote it, or even a programmer at all. Most program users are naive about computers and have no detailed knowledge of a computer's capabilities, limitations and operation. It is vitally important, therefore, that user documentation is accurate, complete, clear and unambiguous.

A representative of the users should be heavily involved in the early stages of the program life cycle in order to provide the analyst with the information he needs about the user's requirements. During the design and coding of the program, the user is involved only infrequently to clarify any problems of ambiguity in the specification. Towards the end of the life cycle, the user may well become involved in testing the program. When the program is finally handed over, the user becomes almost totally dependent on the accompanying user documentation. The quality of the user documentation is even more important for those users who have not been involved in the program's development.

The user documentation must contain all the information necessary to use a program. It should be produced to a high standard of presentation, and provided as a manual or set of manuals. It should contain the following sections.

- *A brief overview of the capabilities of the program*
  This serves to identify the program and to enable a potential user to decide quickly if the program is suitable for his needs. This section should be as short as possible without being vague.
- *A detailed description of the capabilities of the program*
  This description will be broken down into a number of subsections, one subsection per function of the program. The user documentation should be kept at a functional level, and should always avoid detail which is unnecessary to a user. For each of the program's functions, a precise description of input and output data must be provided. There is no need to include a description of how the program produces its results unless the user needs to know which method is being used. For example, in some mathematical or scientific programs, the accuracy of the results will depend on the method used and the user needs to be informed.
- *A complete list of error messages and conditions.*
  When a program cannot produce the expected results because an error is detected during processing, it should produce an appropriate error message. The user documentation should contain a complete list of such error messages, together with an explanation and an indication of what to do to remedy the error. This is particularly important where the user runs the program in an interactive environment.

9.2.3 Programmer documentation

Programmer documentation is used both during the development of the program and after the program has been handed over to the user. It is generated as a by-product of the program development activity and is the main reference document for the development programmer. It also serves as the main source of information for the maintenance programmer, who may have to modify a program he has not written a considerable time after it has gone into use.

While a program is being developed, the programmer can naturally remember quite a lot of detail about the program. To some extent, the development programmer can work with incomplete program documentation. A few months after finishing with a program, however, the programmer's memory will not be so accurate and he will be in essentially the same position as an independent maintenance programmer. Good quality programmer documentation is absolutely vital. If the documentation is bad and a non-trivial modification is needed to a program, it may actually be cheaper to abandon the existing program and write a new one, properly documented, to replace it.

Programmer documentation can be written with the assumption that it will be read by a programmer. What it cannot assume is any familiarity with the program or the particular application. It must be very comprehensive, and would normally contain the following sections.

- *Original specification*
  This should include an outline description of the function of the program and details of any changes agreed by the user.
- *A detailed program structure diagram*
  This should be accompanied by a written explanation for all the design decisions taken.
- *A program listing*
  The program code is perhaps the most important piece of documentation since it is the only part that can be guaranteed to be up-to-date. Standard conventions are normally followed so that the format of coding will assist its readability.
- *Details of testing*
  The testing strategy should be described, together with details of each test data file. Following a modification to the program, the maintenance programmer should follow the same test plan to re-test the program.

9.2.4 Operator documentation

In a batch processing environment, neither the user nor the programmer will be present when the program is run. Instead, this function is performed by the computer operator, and operator documentation must be provided explaining exactly what to do. The operator may have to mount a particular magnetic tape or disc, or load certain pre-printed stationery into the line printer. All the resource requirements of the program must be known if they are to be made available. The expected run-time of the program must be known to help the operator recognise when it has entered an infinite loop.

A list of the messages the program may send, including error messages, is required and precise details of what to do in the case of each of them. In short, the operator documentation must contain a complete and accurate description of the operational characteristics of the program.

When a user runs a program interactively from a terminal, or at a stand-alone microcomputer, operator documentation is still required, though it may be included in the user documentation manual. For instance, a program written for a particular range of microcomputer may well have a requirement for a certain memory size. Similarly, when it is the user who receives the messages relating to unexpected run-time errors, it is the user who must know what to do and whom to contact. This information is essentially operator information but, in the absence of an operator, must be available to the user.

Operator documentation would normally include the following sections.

● *A brief overview of the program*
   This enables the operator to know roughly what the program should do.
● *File identification*
   The operator needs to know which files the program uses so that the appropriate tapes or discs can be located and mounted. The file containing the program itself must be included in this list.
● *Other resource requirements*
   In some cases, it is necessary for the operator to know in advance the memory requirements of the program, the need for special stationery, the expected run-time, the time by which the execution must be completed, the program's priority with respect to other programs, and so on. All these details can be used by the operator to schedule the various programs in a way which maximises the efficiency of the computer.

● *Message details*
   The operator must know precisely how to respond to every message produced by the program. Some messages may simply ask for another file to be mounted, in which case the response is obvious. Other messages may relate to unexpected run-time failures, and the operator needs to know how to react in order to minimise any damage to the files. To cover such eventualities, it is common for operator documentation to contain the telephone number of the person to contact, usually the programmer. The thought of being called out in the middle of the night to correct a program bug only serves to encourage the thorough testing of programs!

9.3 The components of documentation

From the above description it should be clear that documentation must serve as a reference for four different groups of people, and that each group has different requirements of the documentation. Nevertheless, some of these requirements are shared by more than one group and consequently some components of the documentation appear in more than one group's manual. To avoid describing some of the components more than once, descriptions for all the significant components are collected together in this section. Where appropriate, samples of documentation are included after the description of each component. The samples relate to Example 6.3 from Chapter 6.

Brief overview of the program

This should describe, as concisely as possible, the capabilities of the program. The description should be as free of computing jargon as is consistent with the need to be precise.
Sample documentation from Example 6.3.

This program produces a listing from the data held in the Student Records Masterfile. The listing is in three parts:

(1) List of the names of all mature students;
(2) Count of the number of male mature students;
(3) Count of the number of female mature students.

Analysis of requirements

This component describes the original problem and identifies the requirements of the user. In addition, it postulates several possible solutions, where several solutions exist, and provides a cost/benefit analysis for each. Finally, it recommends a particular solution. This document is normally drawn up by the systems analyst and provides the justification for the programming work suggested.
Sample documentation from Example 6.3.

As part of its annual report to the local Education Authority, the college must provide details of the mature students on its courses. In the past, this information has been extracted manually by registry staff examining the application forms of all enrolled students. This has been time-consuming and prone to error.

With the recent computerisation of registration details, and the creation of the Student Records Masterfile, the information can now be produced by the college computer.
Estimated cost of programming effort:

Program design and coding	: 1 man-week
Program testing	: 1 man-week
Documentation	: $\frac{1}{2}$ man-week
Estimated saving of registry staff	: 1 man-week per year

Detailed functional specification

This document provides a description of each of the program's functions, together with a detailed specification of the input and output requirements. This section also contains a complete list of the messages produced by the program whether for data-vetting or error conditions, together with a statement of the necessary reaction.

Sample documentation from Example 6.3.

This program has a single function: to extract information concerning mature students from the Student Records Masterfile.

Input details
One input file is needed: the Student Records Masterfile. This is a standard sequential file where each record has a length of 200 bytes. The fields relevant to this program are detailed below.

Start	End	Type	Range	Description
0	1	Alphanumeric	SR or **	Record type
2	19			Not relevant
20	49	Alphabetic		Surname
50	52	Alphabetic		Initials
53	72			Not relevant
73	74	Numeric	> 16	Age
75	80			Not relevant
81	81	Alphabetic	M or F	Sex
82	199			Not relevant

The first two characters in a record are the record type: SR indicates a student record and ** indicates the trailer record.

Output details
A single line printer file is produced. The first line of output is a standard heading:

MATURE STUDENTS LISTING

Following this, each line contains the name of a mature student (age > 20) extracted from the input file, in the following format.

Start	End	Type	Description
0	9	Alphabetic	Spaces
10	39	Alphabetic	Surname
40	41	Alphabetic	Spaces
42	44	Alphabetic	Initials

Following this list are two lines:

NUMBER OF MALE MATURE STUDENTS IS ****
NUMBER OF FEMALE MATURE STUDENTS IS ****

where **** is a four digit integer, leading zeros suppressed.
Finally, the program produces the following trailer message.

END OF MATURE STUDENTS LISTING

Error messages
The program produces no error messages. No data validation is performed since the Student Records Masterfile is already validated.

Identification of files

The name of each file used by the program should be completely specified here. This may involve identifying not only the file, but also the particular magnetic tape or disc on which the file is held. Besides the main input and output files, any intermediate files (used perhaps to prevent a structure clash) must also be identified.

Detailed program description

The contents of this section vary considerably, depending on the particular approach to program design adopted by the programmer. If the JSP method has been used, this section will contain the data structure diagrams, the outline program structure diagram, the list of actions, and the detailed program structure diagram. It may also contain a *program narrative*: a description in words of the action of the program. Whether the narrative is necessary depends on the quality of the detailed program structure diagram and the readability of the coding.
   Sample documentation from Example 6.3.

Assuming that the program has been developed using JSP, this component of documentation would contain diagrams already given in Chapter 6:

	Figures
Data structure diagrams	6.12,6.15
Outline program structure diagram	6.16,6.17,6.18
List of actions	6.19
Detailed program structure diagram	6.21
Schematic logic	6.25

Development history

This is a description of how the program was designed and implemented. Every non-trivial design decision should be recorded, together with the rationale behind it. The minutes of design team meetings should also be included.

Program listing

This is an up-to-date compiler produced listing of the program. It must not contain any last-minute hand-written alterations; the listing and the actual program must agree. The correct use of standards when coding a program can significantly enhance program documentation; see Section 9.4 for more details.

Sample documentation from Example 6.3.

```
IDENTIFICATION DIVISION.
PROGRAM-ID: MATSTUDLIST.
AUTHOR: JEFF NAYLOR.
DATE-WRITTEN: 10-2-86.
*       THIS PROGRAM PRODUCES A LISTING FROM THE DATA HELD IN
*       THE STUDENT RECORDS MASTERFILE. THE LISTING IS IN
*       THREE PARTS:
*       (1)     A LIST OF THE NAMES OF ALL MATURE STUDENTS;
*       (2)     A COUNT OF THE NUMBER OF MALE MATURE STUDENTS;
*       (3)     A COUNT OF THE NUMBER OF FEMALE MATURE STUDENTS.


ENVIRONMENT DIVISION.
INPUT-OUTPUT SECTION.
FILE-CONTROL.
        SELECT STUD-REC-MAST ASSIGN TO . . .
        SELECT LIST-FILE ASSIGN TO . . .


DATA DIVISION.

FILE SECTION.
*
*       INPUT FILE : STUD-REC-MAST.
*       THE STUDENT RECORDS MASTERFILE. ONLY FIELDS RELEVANT
*       TO THIS PROGRAM HAVE BEEN GIVEN NAMES. REMAINING
*       FIELDS ARE DESCRIBED AS FILLER.
*       FIELD REC-TYPE = SR FOR STUDENT DETAILS RECORDS,
*                      = ** FOR THE TRAILER.
    FD  STUD-REC-MAST
        LABEL RECORDS STANDARD
        DATA RECORD IS STUD-REC.
    01  STUD-REC.
        03      REC-TYPE        PIC XX.
        03      FILLER          PIC X(18).
        03      SURNAME-IN      PIC X(30).
        03      INITIALS-IN     PIC X(3).
        03      FILLER          PIC X(20).
        03      AGE             PIC 99.
        03      FILLER          PIC X(6).
        03      SEX             PIC X.
        03      FILLER          PIC X(118).
*
*       OUTPUT FILE : LIST-FILE.
*       A STANDARD LINE PRINTER FILE. THE RECORD LAYOUT GIVEN
```

```
*      IN LIST-REC IS FOR STUDENT DETAILS LINES.
  FD   LIST-FILE
       LABEL RECORDS STANDARD
       DATA RECORD IS LIST-REC.
  01   LIST-REC.
       03    FILLER            PIC X(10).
       03    OUT-SURNAME       PIC X(30).
       03    FILLER            PIC XX.
       03    OUT-INITIALS      PIC X(3).

  WORKING-STORAGE SECTION.
  01   WS1-HEADER-OUT      PIC X(23)
                   VALUE "MATURE STUDENTS LISTING".
  01   WS2-COUNT-LINE-1.
       03    FILLER             PIC X(36)
                   VALUE "NUMBER OF MALE MATURE STUDENTS IS   ".
       03    WS2-M-COUNT-OUT  PIC ZZZ9.
  01   WS3-COUNT-LINE-2.
       03    FILLER             PIC X(36)
                   VALUE "NUMBER OF FEMALE MATURE STUDENTS IS   ".
       03    WS3-F-COUNT-OUT  PIC ZZZ9.
  01   WS4-TRAILER-OUT      PIC X(30)
                   VALUE "END OF MATURE STUDENTS LISTING".
  01   WS5-ELEMENTARY-FIELDS.
       03    WS5-EOF-FLAG        PIC 9.
       03    WS5-TRAILER-CODE   PIC XX VALUE "**".
       03    WS5-MALE-COUNT      PIC 9(4).
       03    WS5-FEMALE-COUNT  PIC 9(4).

  PROCEDURE DIVISION.

  01-MAT-STUD-PROG.
*      OPEN THE FILES, READ THE FIRST RECORD, INITIALISE
*      COUNTERS AND END-OF-FILE FLAG, AND OUTPUT HEADING.
       OPEN INPUT STUD-REC-MAST
                OUTPUT LIST-FILE.
       READ STUD-REC-MAST, AT END MOVE 1 TO WS5-EOF-FLAG.
       MOVE ZERO TO WS5-MALE-COUNT,
                         WS5-FEMALE-COUNT,
                         WS5-EOF-FLAG.
       WRITE LIST-REC FROM WS1-HEADER-OUT AFTER PAGE.
       MOVE SPACES TO LIST-REC.

  02-PROGRAM-BODY-ITER.
*      CHECK FOR END OF INPUT FILE.
       IF WS5-EOF-FLAG = 1 OR REC-TYPE = WS5-TRAILER-CODE
            GO TO 09-PROGRAM-BODY-END.
  03-STUDENT-REC-SEL.
       IF AGE NOT < 21 GO TO 04-STUDENT-REC-OR.
*      DEAL WITH NON-MATURE STUDENT.
       READ STUD-REC-MAST, AT END MOVE 1 TO WS5-EOF-FLAG.
       GO TO 08-STUDENT-REC-END.
  04-STUDENT-REC-OR.
```

```
*       DEAL WITH MATURE STUDENT.
   05-MAT-STUDENT-SEL.
           IF SEX NOT = "M" GO TO 06-MAT-STUDENT-OR.
*       PROCESS MALE MATURE STUDENT.
           MOVE SURNAME-IN TO SURNAME-OUT.
           MOVE INITIALS-IN TO INITIALS-OUT.
           WRITE LIST-REC AFTER 1.
           ADD 1 TO WS5-MALE-COUNT.
           READ STUD-REC-MAST, AT END MOVE 1 TO WS5-EOF-FLAG.
           GO TO 07-MAT-STUDENT-END.
   06-MAT-STUDENT-OR.
*       PROCESS FEMALE MATURE STUDENT.
           MOVE SURNAME-IN TO SURNAME-OUT.
           MOVE INITIALS-IN TO INITIALS-OUT.
           WRITE LIST-REC AFTER 1.
           ADD 1 TO WS5-FEMALE-COUNT.
           READ STUD-REC-MAST, AT END MOVE 1 TO WS5-EOF-FLAG.
   07-MAT-STUDENT-END.
   08-STUDENT-REC-END.
           GO TO 02-PROGRAM-BODY-ITER.


   09-PROGRAM-BODY-END.
*       OUTPUT STUDENT COUNTS AND TRAILER MESSAGE,
*       CLOSE THE FILES, AND STOP.
           MOVE WS5-MALE-COUNT TO WS2-M-COUNT-OUT.
           WRITE LIST-REC FROM WS2-COUNT-LINE-1 AFTER 3.
           MOVE WS5-FEMALE-COUNT TO WS3-F-COUNT-OUT.
           WRITE LIST-REC FROM WS3-COUNT-LINE-2 AFTER 2.
           WRITE LIST-REC FROM WS4-TRAILER-OUT AFTER 3.
           CLOSE STUD-REC-MAST
                 LIST-FILE.
           STOP RUN.
```

Testing details

This is sometimes known as *acceptance documentation*. It contains a complete history of the testing of the program: a test plan containing the strategy for testing and details of each test run. For each test run there should be listings of the test data, the expected results and the actual results, together with comments on the performance of the program. The test data should not be destroyed; it should be stored on inexpensive media, such as magnetic tape, so that it may be used again if the program needs modifying later. The documentation should contain a reference to the location of the stored data.

Sample documentation from Example 6.3.

```
The program was tested with 7 data files.
(1)  Empty data file
           Data file used          : MAT-STUD-DAT-1
           Expected results file   : MAT-STUD-RES-1
```

(2) Data file with no mature students.
    Data file used   : MAT-STUD-DAT-2
    Expected results file : MAT-STUD-RES-2
(3) Data file with no non-mature students.
    Data file used   : MAT-STUD-DAT-3
    Expected results file : MAT-STUD-RES-3
(4) Data file with some non-mature students and some
  (all male) mature students.
    Data file used   : MAT-STUD-DAT-4
    Expected results file : MAT-STUD-RES-4
(5) Data file with some non-mature students and some
  (all female) mature students.
    Data file used   : MAT-STUD-DAT-5
    Expected results file : MAT-STUD-RES-5
(6) Data file with some non-mature students and some
  (mixed male and female) mature students.
    Data file used   : MAT-STUD-DAT-6
    Expected results file : MAT-STUD-RES-6
(7) The same data file as (6) but with the trailer
  record missing.
    Data file used   : MAT-STUD-DAT-7
    Expected results file : MAT-STUD-RES-7

Operations instructions

In terms of the resources required, this section details the machine environment which must be present for the program to run. It also describes any dialogue that might take place between the operator and the program, specifying the operator's response at each stage.

This list of the components of program documentation is not meant to be exhaustive. The intention was to include all the major items. Figure 9.1 associates each of these components with the various groups of people who would use them.

	Management	Users	Programmers	Operators
Brief overview of the program	●	●	●	●
Analysis of requirements	●			
Detailed functional specification		●	●	
Identification of files		●	●	●
Detailed program description			●	
Development history	●		●	
Program listing			●	
Testing details			●	
Operations instructions		●	●	●

Figure 9.1

9.4 Documentation within the program listing

Many programmers believe that the single most important component of documentation is the program listing. When it becomes necessary to modify an existing program, the circumstances often create significant pressure to perform the modification as quickly as possible. For example, if a run-time error suddenly manifests itself in a program controlling a continuous manufacturing process, such as a beer brewery, or in a program producing the monthly pay-slips, the maintenance programmer will only have a few hours in which to identify, locate and rectify the fault before the customers start complaining. In such circumstances, it is very tempting to defer updating the documentation until more time is available, resulting in much of the documentation becoming out-of-date.

Since the latest listing can be guaranteed to be up-to-date, it is good practice to include in the listing as much documentation as possible. It is true, of course, that when the program code is modified any documentation within the listing must also be modified, but it is easier to do this than it is to up-date documentation manuals and is, therefore, more likely to be done.

Whichever programming language is being used, the programmer should always aim to make the program as readable as possible. All programming languages contain features which the programmer can exploit to make the program self-documenting. The ease with which a programmer can become acquainted with a program written by someone else can be greatly increased if the same coding conventions are adopted by both. Standard coding conventions exist and the vast majority of programmers adhere to them. Unfortunately, the programming profession fails to extract the maximum benefit from the use of such conventions because more than one 'standard' exists. The NCC has established its *Data Processing Documentation Standards* and these are widely used, but with various local deviations.

There are sufficient similarities between the various standards for them to be discussed in terms of *format*, *annotation* and *naming conventions*. Unless specified otherwise, the following conventions apply to both Pascal and COBOL programs.

9.4.1 Format conventions

● Each statement should begin on a new line.
● Blank lines should appear before and after major program components, such as Pascal procedure declarations and COBOL SECTIONs.
● In Pascal, each END should line up with its corresponding BEGIN. The keywords BEGIN and END should appear on a line by themselves.
● In COBOL, paragraph names and section names should appear on a line by themselves.

- Align statements which are at the same level of nesting; use repeated indentation to identify different levels of nesting, and be consistent with indentation.
- Use indentation to show the scope of loops and conditional statements.
- When nesting more than 3 or 4 levels, consider the use of procedures or subroutines instead.

Automatic formatters are available on some computer systems to achieve a standard layout. Usually associated with a particular programming language, a formatter takes unformatted source text and rearranges it into a standard format. This enables the program text to be typed in very quickly, without regard for indentation, but after formatting the text must be carefully checked.

9.4.2 Annotation conventions

- As near the beginning of the program as possible, an explanatory comment should be inserted. This comment should identify the program, the programmer, and the date written. COBOL has specific comment entries for this information. The initial comment should also contain a brief overview of the program and identify the files used. This could be followed by a more detailed specification of the program design, perhaps in the form of schematic logic.
- The beginning of each subroutine, function or procedure in the program should also contain an initial comment detailing its purpose, parameters and method of working.
- Use a comment to identify the end of a subroutine, function or procedure.
- Annotate the coding where necessary to achieve clarity, perhaps by including the relevant schematic logic.
- Do not forget to annotate data definitions. Such a comment could give the range of values for the variable and, where appropriate, the meaning of each value.

9.4.3 Naming conventions

- For every variable or identifier in the program, choose a meaningful name which describes its function. This implies that names will tend to be long but the improvement in readability is significant.
- Try to choose names which imply the location of the definition of a variable. This is particularly important in programs containing a large number of variable definitions. Probably the best way of achieving this is to prefix a name with two or three characters which indicate its location. For example, in a COBOL program, the prefix WS3- could

be used on an identifier defined in the third 01-item in WORKING-STORAGE SECTION. The remainder of the identifier would be a meaningful name.

● The PROCEDURE DIVISION of any non-trivial COBOL program tends to contain a large number of section and paragraph names, and it can be quite difficult to locate in a listing the destination of a particular PERFORM or GO TO statement. This difficulty can be largely removed by adding a numeric prefix to each section and paragraph name and arranging that the prefixes appear in ascending order.

9.5 The provision of documentation

The documentation of a program is not a self-contained stage near the end of the program development cycle. Documentation is generated throughout the program life cycle, often as a by-product of the development stages. Various documents, such as the analysis of requirements and the functional specification, must be produced and approved before the detailed program design can begin. During the development of the detailed program design, documents such as data structure diagrams and action lists will be drawn up. Throughout the testing of the program, details must be kept of each test run so that the programmer's manager can be persuaded to authorise the release of the program to the user. These documents are necessary for successful production of a program; without them the program would not exist.

Other documents, however, are not a necessary by-product of program development and additional effort has to be made to produce them. For example, the development history of a program, detailing all the design decisions, is, inevitably, carried in the programmer's head. To write it all down is an additional burden not gratefully accepted by most programmers. More to the point, writing it down takes valuable time and impedes the program development. This task is best performed by someone else, working in parallel with the programmer. In an environment where regular design progress meetings are held, this task is performed by the minuting secretary.

There are other reasons, of course, why the programmer may not be the best person to produce certain documents. Not all programmers are capable of producing top quality documentation to high standards of presentation. Specific skills are needed for this job, and they are not the same skills as those needed by a programmer to produce programs.

Where a piece of software consists of several programs, it is important that all the programs are documented to the same consistent standards. This argues for one person to produce the formal documentation to enable a consistent style and approach to be used. In fact, documentation plays a very important role in the way a user perceives a piece of software. The documentation is very visible, the software itself is not. The decision to buy one piece of software rather than another is strongly influenced by the quality of the documentation provided. Many software producers now employ specialists to look after the documentation. Such specialists work as full members of the programming team.

During the last few years, there has been some use of the computer itself to produce program documentation. This automated production of documentation has been encouraged by the increased use of standard methods of program development, such as JSP. For example, packages exist which can produce program structure diagrams on a suitable graphics output device. While limited at the moment, the use of such packages is gradually increasing.

9.6 Summary

This chapter has attempted to explain the nature and use of program documentation. The value of good documentation is disputed by hardly anyone, but many object to the cost of producing it. The main problem with documentation is keeping it up-to-date in the face of amendments to the program. The use of documentation specialists has significantly reduced this problem, and also improved the quality of the documentation produced.

CHAPTER 10

The future of programming

10.1 Introduction □ 10.2 Classification of languages □ 10.3 Program design versus coding □ 10.4 Fourth generation languages □ 10.5 Summary

10.1 Introduction

Since at least as far back as the mid-1970s, prophets have been predicting the imminent disappearance of programming. Their argument is that machine capabilities will soon expand to the point where users can instruct computers what to do without going through all the tedious stages of program development. The skilled, and very expensive, services of a professional programmer will not be needed because a user will be able to communicate with the computer in his own language. If the prophets are right, the benefits of studying computing science, and of reading this book, will be short-lived indeed. The apparent reluctance of programming in general, and of languages like COBOL in particular, to simply fade away must be puzzling and even annoying to the prophets.

Nevertheless, important changes have taken place in the nature of the task of programming. This final chapter examines some of the ways in which programming has changed in recent years and suggests possible changes for the future.

10.2 Classification of languages

By the early 1960s, over 30 different computer programming languages were in common use in Britain. By the late 1960s, the figure was well over 100. Since then, this dramatic growth rate has continued. Some languages, notably Algol, have spawned a whole family of different but related languages. In fact, very few languages can claim to be intrinsically new; nearly all languages share common features with each other. Any particular language tends to be strong in those features which best support the type of application for which it was designed. Thousands of programming languages now exist, and in many ways they form a continuous spectrum. Any attempt to provide a classification of programming languages is therefore fraught with difficulties.

It is perhaps easier to identify the characteristics of a good language, whatever the intended area of application.

● The ability to express the solutions to problems in the context of a particular application area, without the need to refer to details of hardware and/or software which are outside this context.
● The ability to express such solutions as compactly as possible while avoiding the lack of clarity which can result from over-compaction.
● The omission of any statements or features which can give rise to ambiguities.
● The ability to express programs in a readable and comprehensible way.
● The inclusion of any notations or conventions which are already accepted standards in the context of the area of application.

Out of necessity, these characteristics are expressed in general terms; such is the breadth of the applications supported by computers. Their common objective, however, is to make the jobs of the programmer and the user easier. They imply very strongly that a language should be designed for a particular application area, and the design should largely ignore the characteristics of the computer on which the programs will run.

This drift from the use of low-level languages to the use of high-level languages is certain to continue in the future. *Problem-orientated* languages enable programs to be developed more quickly and more concisely. They also greatly ease the problems of documentation and maintenance. The only person whose job is made harder by the use of problem-orientated languages is the compiler writer. As the programming language moves further and further away from the computer hardware, the translation task facing the compiler becomes increasingly harder. One consolation for the compiler writer is that hardware designers are continually trying to raise the level of the hardware and close this gap. The compiler writer, however, gets little sympathy from his application programmer colleagues. It is right that the very small number of compiler writers should face these machine problems, and provide the army of application programmers with the high-level tools they need to solve their problems.

10.2.1 The Universal Programming Language

Why is there not just a single *Universal Programming Language*? Apart from the fact that it would make most compiler writers redundant, this notion has great intuitive appeal. Since all programmers would know the same language, the problems of initial coding and subsequent maintenance would be greatly simplified. Programming management would also benefit: all applications software would become portable across different computers and, at machine replacement time, software compatibility would cease to be a constraint on choice. In addition, the adoption of a universal language would encourage the establishment of genuine standards of programming and documentation.

So why has it not happened? There are several reasons for this.

(1)   A language which contains features appropriate to all applications would be enormous. Consequently, the compiler for such a language would also be enormous and most likely slow. The compilation overheads could probably be reduced by writing the compiler in a highly modular fashion, so that those parts of the compiler not invoked by a particular user program need not occupy main memory. The process of compilation is complex, however, and it is not easily broken into independent subtasks; the irreducible part of a compiler tends to be quite large.

(2)   The size problem also has to be faced by programmers. A universal language would be so large that very few programmers would become expert in all aspects of it. In fact, the language would have to be designed in such a way that enabled programmers to learn no more of it than they need for their particular type of problem. It then becomes dubious to claim as universal a language perceived differently by different people.

(3)   Suppliers of computers have a vested commercial interest in making it difficult for a user to switch to a different supplier. One way of achieving this is to make software non-portable: a program written for one machine will not run on a different machine unless exactly the same implementation language is available on both. A user is discouraged from switching supplier if it means rewriting much of his software. A cynic might say that the standardisation of languages like COBOL has been impeded by the commercial interests of the computer manufacturers.

(4)   Another significant impediment to the use of a universal language is general inertia. Programmers would need retraining, and this would require money and effort. While languages such as COBOL and FORTRAN can meet 90% of our needs, there is little short-term incentive to change. In any event, COBOL and FORTRAN programmers would still be needed for a considerable time in order to

maintain the huge number of existing programs.

10.3 Program design versus coding

It is important not to confuse program design with coding. Program design starts with the functional specification of the program and a detailed specification of input and output data; program design finishes with the production of the detailed program structure diagram. Coding is the conversion of the detailed program structure diagram into the statements of a particular programming language. Traditionally, these two tasks within the program development cycle have been performed by the same person, but this is not the only way to organise a programming team.

Program design, as defined above, is the more skilled of the two tasks. The production of a good program design usually requires extensive experience and a high level of natural ability. Even with the assistance of a systematic programming method such as JSP, program design is a highly creative task. By comparison, coding is much simpler, almost mechanical, in nature. Coding usually involves applying fairly straightforward techniques to the program structure diagram, or schematic logic, in order to produce the program code. It requires, of course, a detailed knowledge of the implementation language but, in general, does not require as much experience or natural ability as program design.

Many programming team managers separate the two tasks and allocate them to different people within the team. Senior programmers are asked to produce program designs; these are then given to junior programmers to code. Of course, the division of labour is not quite this clear. Particularly difficult or critical programs may well be coded by a senior programmer. Having gained some experience, a junior programmer who shows the ability will be asked to produce program designs for the more straightforward programs. This separation of program design from coding enables the programming team manager to use his staff in the most cost-effective way. The most difficult tasks are performed by the most able people, who usually are paid the most money.

10.3.1 Automatic code generation

This identification of coding as a separable task has led in recent years to the development of *automatic code generators*. These are software packages which take a program design, specified in some suitable formal notation, and produce the corresponding code.

The fundamental problem is to 'execute' a program design on a particular set of computer hardware. In theory at least, automatic code generators can work in various ways.

Interpretation of the program design

The program design must specify the actions to be performed, the conditions to be evaluated, and the path of execution. Thus, by itself it is a high-level language. If it is expressed in a machine-readable form, as is the case with schematic logic, it can be treated like any other high-level programming language. One of the ways of executing it would be via an *interpreter*. This is a piece of software which examines the program design statement by statement, and obeys the statement by interpreting the actions it contains. This form of direct execution is very slow and is not really practical for frequently-run programs. In fact, execution by interpretation involves no code generation at all; the program design is executed directly. The interpreter itself could be written in any language with good text manipulation facilities. If the interpreter were written in a high-level language, it would be fairly portable between different computers but would slow down the execution of the user program even more. If the interpreter were written in a low-level language, it would be fairly efficient but would obviously be machine-dependent; a different interpreter would be needed for each machine.

Generation of machine code

The automatic code generator could perform the functions of a complete compiler and produce executable machine code as its output. The user program would then be executed at full machine speed, many times faster than under an interpreter. The code generator would face all the problems of high-level language compilers. It is likely to be a fairly large piece of software and be quite expensive to develop. Because it produces machine code, it would clearly be machine-dependent; a different code generator would be needed for each different machine.

Generation of high-level language code

This approach avoids most of the problems faced by a full compiler by tackling a smaller task. The program design is translated into a standard high-level language for which a compiler is already available. This high-level language program is then compiled in the normal way to produce machine code. This two-stage code generation is shown diagrammatically in Figure 10.1.

Figure 10.1

This approach has several advantages. The user program runs at normal speed. The code generator itself is portable across all computers that support the language into which it translates the program design. The code generator need not concern itself much with syntax errors in the program design specification; it can rely on the normal syntax checking of the compiler to validate the generated code.

Interpretation of the program design is normally discounted because of the severe degradation of speed experienced when executing a program under an interpreter. Generation of machine code involves the development of large and costly code generators which can only run on a single computer, and is therefore normally discounted. Generation of high-level language code is by far the most attractive proposition and several code generators of this type are available.

All three methods depend on the program design being expressed in a formal, machine-readable notation. JSP program structure diagrams are an excellent visual way of describing a program structure, but are unsuitable as input to a code generator. JSP schematic logic, however, is suitable and several code generators make use of it. A *JSP preprocessor* is a software package which takes a form of schematic logic and produces the corresponding program in a standard high-level language, usually COBOL. Most of these packages only deal with the PROCEDURE DIVISION, the other three divisions are left to the programmer to generate in the traditional way. Included in such packages, or perhaps accompanying them, there is often a syntax checker which validates the schematic logic before it is used for code generation.

The use of automatic code generators relieves the programmer of much of the tedium and monotony of coding. It also holds many attractions for the programming team manager. Code generators can produce code more quickly than people. They are also more accurate and do not become error-prone when tired. They are willing to work long, unsociable hours and have never been known to ask for a rise in salary! More seriously, they cost less than human coders. Their use is likely to continue.

10.3.2 Report generators

Whenever a program is written, there is an element of 'reinventing the wheel'. Almost always, the problem to be solved, or at least one very similar to it, has already been solved by someone else. Indeed, certain problems are solved so frequently that, when viewed on a national scale, it is a gross misuse of human and machine resources to start afresh each time.

A report program is an example of a program which, with minor variations, is written many, many times throughout the computing industry. A report program produces a listing of the contents of a file. The report will probably not contain the complete contents of a file; for example, a report of all employees over retiring age may be needed, and this could be extracted from the complete employee file. Similarly, it may be necessary to perform simple calculations on the input file data in order to produce extra fields for the report. Such report programs are usually written in COBOL and are very similar to each other.

A *report generator* is a package which accepts a description of the requirements for a particular report and produces the appropriate report program in source COBOL form. This can then be compiled and run in the normal way. The generated COBOL program will have a standard structure but its conditions and action list will vary according to the particular report required. When using a report generator, the programmer must provide

- Details of the input file, including field sizes and field locations
- Details of the report file, giving the locations of the fields copied across from the input file
- Conditions which are used to select certain input file records
- Details of calculations to be performed
- Details of report headings and footings, page headings and footings, and so on.

Report generators have been in use for many years. They represent one of the first attempts to reduce the duplication of programming effort. Instead of writing the COBOL program, the programmer provides the parameters to the report generator package. This approach has been used with other frequently-needed application programs, such as sort and merge programs, and its use is likely to increase.

10.3.3 The provision of software

When a user decides to solve a particular problem by using a piece of software, the best means of providing that software must be determined. Fundamentally, the user has three choices.

(1) It can be written by the user himself, or, more likely, the user can delegate it to one of his own programmers. The speed at which the software is produced, and to some extent its quality, will then depend on the amount of company resources the user allocates to the job. No non-trivial program can be produced overnight, and this choice commits the user to the normal delays inherent in the production of new software. If the required piece of software is large, or beyond the capabilities of his existing staff, the user may have to employ extra programming staff on a temporary basis. At least with this approach, the user remains in total control of the software development and should be able to provide adequate maintenance later on.

(2) The user can pay someone else to write it. If the piece of software

requires special techniques which are beyond the experience of the user's own programmers, an outside agency could be contracted to produce the software. Independent consultants or software houses provide these services. The software is unlikely to be produced much more quickly, and may well cost more, than if it was produced by the user himself. With this approach, the user must make adequate arrangements for maintenance support once the software has been handed over.

(3)   The user can buy a standard package to do the job. If the user is faced by a fairly common commercial or industrial problem, it is likely that a standard package already exists to solve it. The user could simply buy the package and avoid all the development delay. If the package does not exactly fit the user's particular problem, the problem can be changed to fit the package, or the user can pay to have the package tailored to his precise needs. In order to cover as many applications as possible, packages tend to be written in a general way, and they are invariably less efficient than purpose-built software. When buying a package, the user normally frees himself from maintenance problems; the package supplier likes to remain responsible for its maintenance in order to protect the package from unauthorised amendment.

The user must carefully evaluate the advantages and disadvantages of each means of software provision. The user's eventual choice will be based on a large number of factors: cost, speed, the need for security, past experience, and so on.

10.4 Fourth generation languages

During the last few years, several trends have been emerging in software production.

(1)   Many companies admit to a backlog in programming system development, of the order of two or three years. This is not the delay between starting and finishing a particular program; it is the delay between requesting a program and work on that program actually starting.

(2)   There is a shortage of skilled systems analysts and programmers and this shortage is severely impeding the development of new systems.

(3)   Far too much of the scarce programming resource is used up in maintaining existing programs. Some estimates put the figure as high as 70%.

(4)   The range of applications of computers is expanding more rapidly than ever before, and user software requirements are changing rapidly as a consequence. Traditional methods of program development cannot

keep pace.

(5) Computer literacy has increased the desire of many users to become more directly involved in the development of their computer-based systems.

These problems have led to intense demand for ways to increase the productivity of programmers and to reduce program development time. In Section 10.3.2 it was seen how this has been partly achieved through the use of report generators. The last few years have seen the rapid development of this approach and the introduction of *Fourth Generation Languages* or 4GLs.

Unfortunately, there is no standard definition of a fourth generation language. Worse than this, there are many products now available which claim to be fourth generation languages but are clearly and intrinsically different from each other. To some extent, the suppliers of these products are jumping on the 4GL bandwagon, hoping that the name will boost their sales.

In general terms, a 4GL is a computer-based language in which the programmer, or even the user, specifies only *what* is to be done and not *how* to do it. The specification of what is to be done is written in a ultra-high-level English-like language, for example

PRINT EMPLOYEE NAMES OVER RETIRING AGE

Improvements in programmer productivity are dramatic; factors of 10:1 and even 20:1 are claimed and achieved. Program development time is vastly improved. 4GLs are designed to be friendly and easy to use; the user can program them himself without the assistance of a specialist programmer; training to use a 4GL is said to take one or two days. Programs written in a 4GL are so short (perhaps one-twentieth of the size of a corresponding COBOL program) and easy to amend that maintenance problems and the need for detailed programmer documentation are significantly reduced. Many 4GLs automatically produce their own documentation.

At first sight, 4GLs seem to offer the answer to many problems. However, they are still very much in the development stage. For most 4GLs, the range of application is fairly limited; they are written for a particular type of problem in a specific environment. Some of the product-types claimed to be fourth generation languages are listed below.

- Database query languages
- Information retrieval systems
- Report writers
- Spreadsheets
- Application generators

- Very high-level programming languages
- Screen painters
- Prototyping languages

Since these product-types are quite distinct from each other, it is difficult to refer to them all as fourth generation languages, and in any case many of them are much more than simply a language. Increasingly, each product-type is being referred to as a *fourth generation tool*. Some fourth generation products actually contain more than one fourth generation tool.

Traditional programming system development has involved the user at an early stage in specifying his requirements and approving the functional specification. The user then plays no further part while systems analysts and programmers busy themselves with program design, coding and testing. When the final product is ready, the user is brought back in to approve the testing and accept the product. At this stage, it is quite common for the user to realise that the product is not quite what he wants.

There are several possible reasons for this. The user's requirements may have changed in the time taken to develop the program. There may have been a communication problem between the systems analyst and the user. The analyst may not have properly understood the user's needs. The user may not have properly understood what the analyst was offering. Whatever the cause, changing the program at a very late stage will certainly be expensive; it may even be impossible.

Fourth generation languages help to avoid this problem by reducing program development time so much that user requirements are unlikely to change, and by expressing the program in a form that the user can understand, enabling the user to become deeply involved throughout the program's development. The possibility of misunderstanding is almost removed.

Development times are so reduced that *prototyping* is a sensible and practical course of action. This involves building quickly and simply a working approximation to the final system, omitting much of the detail. The objective is to refine the overall structure of the program and files. The prototype may be developed in a special *prototyping language*, designed for ease of construction and modification. Alternatively, the prototype may be developed in the language chosen for the final version. Once the user has approved the prototype, detailed work can begin on the final version. Prototyping has been used for several years in the traditional program development cycle, but its cost has always restricted its widespread use. 4GLs will reduce development costs to the point where the use of prototyping will become standard.

10.5 Summary

Making predictions about the future of programming is a dangerous pastime. No one knows what will happen; only guesses can be made based on current developments and trends. Certainly, the number of low-level programmers is dwindling rapidly; even systems software, such as an operating system, is now commonly written in a high-level language. The traditional high-level languages such as COBOL have also lost some of their attraction as the software crisis has deepened. Fourth generation languages appear to offer the way forward, together with the increased use of prototyping.

Some pundits have been too hasty in predicting the demise of the computer programmer. The increased use of 4GLs heralds dramatic changes in the programmer's job. The programmer will use new tools and techniques to develop ever larger and more complex software systems. The best way a programmer can prepare himself to meet the challenges of tomorrow is by ensuring that he fully understands the fundamentals of the craft that he practises today.

Index

acceptance documentation 196
accuracy 72
actual parameter list 111
address error 103
admit 183, 184
algorithms 28
analysis of requirements 191, 200
annotation conventions 198, 199
arithmetic overflow 72, 73
arithmetic underflow 73
arithmetic unit 6
applications software 14
assembler 13
assembly language 12
automatic formatters 199
automatic generation 205
automatic generators 205, 206, 207

backing storage 6
backtracking 179, 180, 182, 183
batch 18
batch processing systems 17
binary search 89
binary tree 156, 157, 158, 161
black box testing 109, 110
blocks 9
Boolean 75, 78, 79, 88
bottom, 138
boundary clashes 167, 169, 170
bug 102, 106, 107
buffer 9

cascade selection 61, 62
central processing unit (CPU) 5
character 75
character codes 76

character set 75
character string 75, 77
code generation 206
code generator 206, 207
coding 25
coding conventions 198
collating sequence 76
command language 16
  (see job control language)
compiler 14
compound statement 43
computational errors 17
condition names 79
context editors 21
control unit 6
correctness 29
correspondence 123, 124, 166, 167, 168, 169, 170
counter-controlled crop 45, 47, 48
cross-reference listing 107

data 3
data structure 79, 82, 83, 120, 137, 170
data structure diagrams 200
debugging 102, 103, 104, 105, 106, 110
debugging aids 106
debugging line 105
debugging phase 102
design 25
desk checking 97, 106, 107
diagnostic messages 101, 102
documentation 96, 106
dry run 97
dry running 97, 107

ease of use 30
echo-printing 111
efficiency 30
end-order tree-traversal 161, 162
error correction 106
error location 104
exponent 69, 70

field 9, 162, 163, 164
files 3, 163, 164, 168, 169, 171, 174,
    179, 180, 181, 184, 190, 192
First In First Out (FIFO) 149
floating point 70, 71, 74
flowchart 31
formal parameter list 111
format conventions 198
formatter 21, 199
fourth generation tool 211
fourth generator language 210, 211,
    212
free list 145, 147, 157
frequency analysers 107
"friendliness" 30
front 149
functional specification 192, 200,
    205, 211

hashed random file 164
head 143, 146
high-level languages 13
hypothesis 182, 183

icons 75
immediate access storage 5
implementation 25
in-line 49, 54
in-order tree-transversal 161, 162
indexed sequential file 164
infinite loop 45
information 3
integer 67, 68, 71, 72
interactive systems 17
interactive testing systems 107, 108
intermediate file 168, 169, 170, 171,
    173, 174, 176
interpreters 206, 207
iteration 32, 34, 37

JSP structure diagrams 115, 118,
    120, 207

language translator 14

Last In First Out (LIFO) list 138
leading decision loops 42, 47, 49, 51,
    53, 65
leaf nodes 156
left subtree 157
level-88 condition-names 78
linear list 137, 138, 142, 144, 145,
    149, 157
linear search 87, 89
linked lists 142, 143, 144, 145, 146,
    152, 153, 157
logging in/logging on 19
logging off 20
logging out 20
logical 137
logical data structures 136, 164
logic error 106
logical error 102, 103
logical operators 79
loop control variable 45, 47, 48, 49,
    50, 51, 111
loss of significance 74
low-level languages 12

machine code 206
machine code instructions 11
maintainability 30
management-documentation 187
mantissa 69, 70
MAXINT 68
meaningful name 199, 200
merging 87, 91
milestones 187
modular programming 114
module 114
multi-dimensional arrays 83
multiple read-ahead 179
multiple read-ahead technique 180

naming conventions 198, 199
narrative diagrams 193
nested loops 53, 54, 58
nesting 53, 54, 55, 61
nested selection 59, 62, 63, 64, 65
node 143, 144, 145, 147, 153, 155,
    156, 157, 158, 159, 161, 164
non-numeric data 67, 75
non-sequential mapping 138, 142,
    152
normal operation and
    maintenance 26
numeric data 67, 75

one-dimensional array   77, 83, 86, 87, 89
one-pass problems   171
operating systems   15
operator documentation   189, 190
or   183
order clashes   167, 171
order code processor (OCP)   5
ordered serial file   164
out-of-line   49, 58
output files   170
overflow   72
overview   188, 190, 191, 199

physical data structures   136, 137, 164
popping   140, 142
portability   30
posit   183, 184
post-order traversal   162
power-per-cubic-foot (pcf)   5
pre-order tree-traversal   161
problem-orientated   203
program counter   6
program documentation   201
program inversion   171, 172, 176, 179
program life-cycle   187, 188, 200
program listing   189, 198
program narrative   193
program structures   120, 123, 126, 132, 172, 179, 181
program structure diagram   189, 193, 201, 205, 207
program traces   107
prototyping   211, 212
prototyping language   211
pseudocode   32
pushing   139, 142

queues   138, 149, 150, 151, 152, 153, 154, 164
quit   183, 184

read-ahead   46, 132, 175, 179
real   67, 69, 70, 71, 72, 73, 74, 75
rear   149
recognition problems   166, 179, 180, 182, 183, 184
record   8, 162, 163, 164, 168, 169, 171, 176, 179, 180, 181
recursion   58
recursive   111, 159
recursive definition   155, 156
recursive procedure   159, 161

report generator   207, 208, 210
report program   207, 208
representation   74
representation error   72, 74
right subtree   157
root   155, 156, 157

schematic   132, 134, 173, 175, 176, 182, 183, 199, 205, 207
scientific notation   69, 70
screen editors   21
searching   87
sel   183
selection   32, 33, 36
semantic errors   102
sequence   32, 33, 36
sequence register   6
sequential file   164
sequential mapping   138, 139, 142, 149, 152
serial file   163, 164
side effects   183
singly linked list   143
software   14
software houses   15
software package   15
sorting   87, 89, 158
specification   25
stacks   138, 139, 140, 141, 142, 145, 146, 147, 148
stack overflow   139, 141, 142, 145, 149, 154, 164
stack underflow   140
stepwise refinement   35, 41, 54
storage maps   107
structure clashes   166, 167, 168, 170, 171
structure diagram   35, 40, 54, 55, 59, 61, 88, 89, 90, 91, 92, 93, 118, 120, 121
structured programming   41, 65, 176
subscript   79, 81, 82, 84, 87, 88
syntax   98, 99, 100, 101, 102, 207
syntax diagrams   98, 99, 100
syntex errors   98, 101, 102
systems software   14

test   108
test data   108, 109
test data generators   109
testing   26, 95, 96, 108, 109, 110, 111, 112
three dimensional array   83

top   138
trailing decision loops   51, 52, 53, 65
trees   155, 156, 158, 159, 160, 161,
   164
tree-traversal   161
tree-walk   161
truncation   69, 71, 72, 74
turnaround time   18
two dimensional arrays   83, 84, 87
two pass problems   171

underflow   74

universal language   24, 204
Universal Programming Language 204
user documentation   187, 188
utility programs   15

vectors   79, 83, 84
Visual Display Unit (VDU)   10

walkthrough   97, 98, 107
white box testing   110